THE MAGIC OF POSITIVE THINKING

THE MAGIC OF POSITIVE THINKING

HARNESSING THE POWER WITHIN

ROGER FRITZ

RUPA

Published by
Rupa Publications India Pvt. Ltd 2024
7/16, Ansari Road, Daryaganj
New Delhi 110002

Sales centres:
Bengaluru Chennai
Hyderabad Jaipur Kathmandu
Kolkata Mumbai Prayagraj

P-ISBN: 978-93-5702-874-5
E-ISBN: 978-93-5702-964-3

First impression 2024

10 9 8 7 6 5 4 3 2 1

Printed in India

CONTENTS

1. Positive Attitude—the Key to Success 7
2. Interpreting Your World 21
3. Upgrading Capabilities 48
4. Overcoming Problems Together 78
5. Motivating Others 93
6. Conquering Burnout and Stress 138
7. Effective Leaders Are Positive 150
8. Maximizing Your Performance 167
9. Sharpening Your Interpersonal Skills 181
10. How Attitude Affects Results 188

1

POSITIVE ATTITUDE—THE KEY TO SUCCESS

'Things turn out best for the people who make the best of the way things turn out.'

—John Wooden

Upon contemplation of your approach to both life and work, a profound realization dawns—beyond its impact on achievements, a positive attitude stands as a formidable shield against burnout while concurrently acting as a catalyst for skill enrichment. It's the cornerstone that shapes the landscape for success, paving the way for those poised to seize triumphs.

The ripple effect of a positive attitude extends to the realm of success. Its essence lies in the genuine appreciation for existing blessings, a shield against the grip of despondency stemming from unfulfiled desires. Essentially, attitude stands as the propellant driving endeavours, whether within the confines of committee service or the quest for commanding positions within sprawling multinational corporations. It fuels the ambition to carve success in business domains, render service to humanity through various professions or contribute to life's magnificence via artistic expression.

At the crux of accomplishment lies the unwavering commitment to pursue defined objectives, propelled by individual prowess. At times, it mandates reliance solely on oneself—a testament to the verity that one's progress hinges upon their resolve. Success epitomizes the evolution from mere acceptability to the realm of sheer excellence—a path rarely trodden without rigorous toil and steadfast dedication.

The journey toward excellence typically unfurls along a demanding path of arduous apprenticeship, where the crucible of experience melds raw potential into refined prowess. To enhance the likelihood of hard work culminating in the realization of one's aspirations, a repertoire of indispensable personal attributes emerges as pivotal:

- Self-esteem stands as the bedrock upon which all aspirations rest. The perception of oneself as a valuable, capable individual becomes the cornerstone for effecting change and orchestrating control over the ebbs and flows of opportunities presented by life's tapestry.
- Responsibility emerges as a guiding principle, woven intricately into the fabric of one's existence. Embracing the mantle of accountability for every twist and turn, whether leading to triumph or tribulation, underscores the essence of personal agency in shaping destiny.
- Optimism thrives as the beacon lighting the way amidst the tumultuous seas of uncertainty. It necessitates an unwavering belief in the potential for success, notwithstanding the recognition that certain circumstances may lie beyond immediate influence. Success burgeons within those who harbour self-assurance, exude confidence in the prospects of the future and labour diligently in the present.
- Steady progress epitomizes the art of measured

advancement—a progression measured meticulously, step by deliberate step. Visionaries of success keep their goals emblazoned in their sights, not merely as benchmarks of accomplishment but as motivational signposts directing their present actions while charting the course for future endeavours.

- Imagination serves as the fertile ground wherein the seeds of innovation and new vistas take root before they sprout into reality. The imaginative prowess of successful individuals transcends boundaries, weaving the fabric of possibilities and nurturing unconventional ideas.
- Awareness unfolds as an unceasing sentinel, attuned to the rhythms of the world. Those who succeed exude a relentless curiosity, their perceptive gaze ever fixed upon the horizon of new opportunities, ever-ready to seize the fleeting chances that beckon.
- Creativity, a catalyst for metamorphosis, urges the mind to wander beyond conventional confines. The trailblazers of success habitually traverse uncharted territories, probing problems and opportunities from myriad perspectives. They challenge conventions, perpetually questioning the 'what', 'how', 'when', and 'who', in pursuit of innovation and evolution.

'Always bear in mind that your own resolution to succeed is more important than any other one thing.'

—Abraham Lincoln

CRITERIA FOR SUCCESSFUL LEADERS

The dichotomy between sidestepping failure and actively pursuing success is starkly evident in the trajectory of leaders like Lee Iacocca, whose indomitable spirit and unwavering positivity stand as a testament to transcending adversities. His ascendancy to the helm of Chrysler Motors epitomized the embodiment of a leader willing to embrace the gambit of failure in pursuit of monumental triumphs.

Iacocca's persona radiated an unyielding tenacity and an unflinching resolve, palpable not just in boardroom discussions but also resonating through the airwaves in vivid television commercials championing his company's cause. His leadership style echoed a pragmatism and a resolute determination encapsulated by the credo, 'Let's confront reality and forge ahead.' These traits became the cornerstone of his leadership at Chrysler, traits he sought fervently when assembling his top-tier team.

In the mosaic of Iacocca's candid evaluations, the paragons of success within Chrysler were painted with hues of grit, resilience and forthrightness. His candid, often colourful descriptions encapsulated the essence of individuals who thrived under his tutelage. They were individuals characterized by:

- Risk-Taking Mavericks: the trailblazers of progress, possess a calculated audacity that propels them into uncharted territories. They're unafraid to stake their professional standing for the pursuit of pioneering endeavours. Their appetite for innovation drives them to champion untested yet crucial projects, understanding that true progress often requires pushing beyond conventional boundaries, even at the expense of personal security.
- Controlled Workaholics: exhibit an insatiable thirst for challenge and excitement within their roles, transcending the conventional confines of a typical workday. Their commitment to accomplishment supersedes the mere tally

of hours clocked in. Their passion fuels an unrelenting dedication to their craft, where the thrill of achievement supersedes the constraints of time, becoming the ultimate reward.

- Honest Communicators: characterized by their fearlessness in voicing their convictions, navigate the landscape of dialogue with a blend of boldness and sincerity. They articulate their vision in a manner that galvanizes action, fostering an environment where open, reciprocal communication thrives. Their clarity of expression and unwavering commitment to factual feedback forge a foundation for constructive interaction.
- Fearless Delegators: exemplify a rare courage in entrusting significant responsibilities to their team members, fostering an environment where autonomy and accountability flourish. By leading through example, they inspire others to strive for excellence, granting space for individuals to thrive or learn from failures autonomously.
- Practical Planners: possess a visionary acumen that allows them to perceive the entirety of a task rather than approaching it piecemeal. They wield foresight as a tool, systematically setting priorities and delineating a roadmap for progress. Their methodical approach to planning ensures comprehensive execution and accurate gauging of advancement.
- Tough-Minded Decision-Makers: exhibit an unwavering resolve to make tough calls, unhampered by sentimental attachments. They prioritize the collective good, swiftly discarding redundant or inefficient programs and making pragmatic choices, even if it involves replacing long-standing employees to optimize team efficiency and effectiveness.

- Dreamers with Common Sense: tread the fine line between visionary thinking and practical outcomes. Their dreams are welcomed, provided they materialize into tangible results within reasonable timeframes. Performance becomes the litmus test, emphasizing tangible achievements over lofty aspirations.
- Sacrificial Performers: embody a reservoir of boundless energy and dedication, consistently surpassing expectations. Their enthusiasm becomes infectious, igniting motivation in others. Despite encountering limited encouragement, their unwavering resolve steers them onward, directing their energy with precision and resilience, a testament to their unwavering commitment to the task at hand.

THE ATTRIBUTES OF WINNERS

Winners, astute in their interpersonal dynamics, anchor their relationships on a foundation fortified by four pivotal principles, each serving as a compass guiding their interactions:

The cornerstone principle revolves around the belief that everyone harbours motivational triggers waiting to be uncovered. Dispelling the notion that certain individuals are inherently devoid of motivation, winners recognize the imperative of identifying these unique motivational keys early on. Managers, in particular, bear the onus of delving into these psychological nuances, decoding what inspires and fuels each individual within their purview. This proactive approach becomes instrumental in unlocking the latent potential and enthusiasm, paving the way for a more engaged and productive workforce.

Another cardinal principle underscores the intrinsic truth that people are predominantly driven by their own aspirations, not necessarily aligned with external directives. Winners adeptly navigate this reality, striving to unearth the intrinsic motivations propelling individuals forward. This entails an empathetic exploration into the personal motivations and aspirations of team members, aligning these intrinsic drivers with the goals of the organization. By intertwining personal aspirations with professional tasks, a harmonious synergy emerges, empowering individuals to work with zeal, driven by intrinsic desires.

Moreover, winners acknowledge the individuality of concerns and perspectives within their teams. They realize the need to address these concerns conscientiously, integrating them into the fabric of task assignments. By acknowledging and incorporating these personal concerns into the professional landscape, winners foster an environment of inclusivity and consideration, catalysing greater commitment and ownership from team members.

Furthermore, winners understand that effective leadership and relationship-building hinge on the art of effective communication. They cultivate an environment where open dialogue thrives, nurturing an atmosphere where team members feel heard, understood and valued. This not only bridges the gap between leadership objectives and individual motivations but also fortifies the bonds of trust and understanding within the organizational framework.

Winners in the realm of relationship management exhibit a profound understanding of the multifaceted nature of motivation, individual aspirations, and the indispensability of empathetic communication. They deftly weave these threads together, fashioning a tapestry of relationships that fosters a culture of mutual respect, understanding and collective drive toward shared objectives.

The third principle underscores the nuanced understanding

that an exaggerated emphasis on a strength can paradoxically transform it into a liability. An illustrative example resonates vividly: Carl Adams, a client and president of an organization, exemplified an unwavering commitment to punctuality. His unwavering belief that early arrivals heralded the most valuable contributions became an entrenched perspective. However, this fixation on punctuality morphed into an overshadowing force, eclipsing the actual substance of contributions. The fervour for promptness superseded the evaluation of recommendations, culminating in a skewed hierarchy where the timing of arrival usurped the merit of ideas. While punctuality is commendable, its excessive pursuit at the expense of content quality inevitably leads to flawed judgments and overlooks valuable insights.

Furthermore, the fourth principle espouses the profound truth that true motivation emanates from within, nurtured by an environment conducive to self-driven action. Effective leaders comprehend that their role transcends merely dangling rewards as incentives. Instead, they embark on the arduous quest of crafting an ecosystem that nurtures and inspires self-motivation among their teams. Rather than incessantly relying on external motivators, leaders sow the seeds of autonomy, trust and empowerment within their organizational fabric. This strategic cultivation fosters a culture where individuals feel empowered to take initiative, make decisions and drive their own progress, even in the absence of constant supervision.

In essence, the third principle highlights the necessity of balancing strengths, ensuring they enhance rather than eclipse other essential facets of decision-making. While the fourth principle underscores the transformative power of creating a self-motivating environment, recognizing that sustained motivation arises not solely from external incentives but from the cultivation of an internal drive catalysed by an empowering and nurturing organizational culture. By harmonizing these principles, leaders forge a path towards balanced and effective leadership, fostering an environment that values contributions beyond mere timeliness and cultivates self-motivated individuals driven by intrinsic passion and purpose.

ENTHUSIASM IS CONTAGIOUS

Enthusiasm stands as a beacon of positivity, radiating its influence far and wide within any setting:

Tommy Lasorda, renowned for his vibrant spirit as the manager of the Los Angeles Dodgers, embodies the belief that enthusiasm is not merely a personal attribute but a contagion that permeates entire environments. His conviction in the contagious nature of attitude resonates profoundly: within the confines of a sports clubhouse or the walls of an office, the demeanour of leaders serves as the barometer for the collective attitude of their teams.

Lasorda's analogy draws a vivid parallel between a leader's attitude and its ripple effect within the team. He elucidates the palpable impact of his own demeanour on team morale, highlighting the transformative power of a leader's disposition. A leader's arrival into a workspace, whether draped in despondency or brimming with enthusiasm and confidence, sets the tone for the entire environment. The contagion effect becomes evident as the prevailing mood echoes the leader's emotional state. The infectious nature of enthusiasm transcends boundaries, uplifting spirits and fostering a culture of optimism and energy.

Furthermore, Lasorda's insights extend beyond the immediate influence of attitude; he intricately weaves the concept of loyalty into the fabric of organizational dynamics. For Lasorda, loyalty is a reciprocal relationship—fueled by the reciprocal exchange of dedication and appreciation. He draws a direct correlation between fostering a deep-rooted love for one's work and the ensuing pride that fuels exceptional performance. His poignant query about the rarity of individuals fervently desiring a lifelong association with their organizations posthumously underscores the essence of fostering a work environment that nurtures loyalty and dedication.

In essence, Lasorda's wisdom unveils the symbiotic relationship between attitude and the organizational ethos. Leaders, by embodying enthusiasm and optimism, wield an influential power that transcends individual sentiments, shaping the collective morale and productivity. Moreover, his emphasis on reciprocal loyalty serves as a poignant reminder of the imperative of fostering a workplace culture where dedication, pride and love for work thrive, birthing an ecosystem where loyalty and exceptional performance become the bedrock of success.

'You are as young as your faith
As old as your doubts
As young as your self confidence
As old as your fears
As young as your hope
As old as your despair.
Years may wrinkle the skin
But to give up enthusiasm
Wrinkles the soul.'

—Samuel Ullman

The role of attitude in leadership is pivotal, exerting a profound influence on organizational dynamics and progress. Effective leaders adeptly navigate the correlation between attitude and behaviour, leveraging this understanding to propel organizations forward. Their actions are guided by a vision that promotes mutual benefit, fostering an environment where success is not just individual but collective.

One fundamental truth elucidated by effective leaders is the reciprocity inherent in nurturing success. They comprehend that by empowering and facilitating the success of their team members, a culture of collaboration and support flourishes. This ethos of assistance reciprocates, fostering a harmonious environment where collective achievements become the norm. Conversely, erecting barriers or impeding progress sets a precedent for discord, fostering an environment where retaliatory actions become prevalent, hindering overall productivity.

Respect emerges as a cornerstone in the leader-employee dynamic. Leaders who earn respect wield a powerful tool for fostering cooperation and minimizing hostility within their teams. By nurturing an environment where respect is mutual, effective leaders mitigate conflicts and pave the way for smoother collaboration and innovation.

Furthermore, effective leaders eschew the use of humiliating assignments or directives, recognizing their propensity to rebound unfavourably. Such actions tend to backfire, resulting in resentment and often manifesting as counterproductive behaviour during critical junctures.

These leaders also prioritize meritocracy, valuing results over mere agreeability. Rather than favouring those who echo their sentiments, they recognize and reward individuals based on their tangible contributions and the outcomes they deliver. This ethos of recognizing and rewarding efficacy fosters an environment that encourages genuine feedback and diverse perspectives.

Moreover, effective leaders understand the distinction between seeking popularity and earning respect. While popularity might be fleeting, respect breeds enduring allegiance and commitment. Their focus lies not on garnering gratitude but on fostering an environment where respect becomes the cornerstone of relationships.

Additionally, they anchor their leadership on trust and accountability, delivering on commitments and avoiding overpromising. Encouraging participation in goal-setting instills a sense of ownership and commitment among team members, driving collective efforts towards shared objectives.

In essence, effective leaders understand that attitude, as manifested through their actions and decisions, shapes the organizational culture and dynamics. By embracing principles centred on mutual benefit, respect, fairness and accountability, they foster an environment where collaboration thrives, enabling sustained growth and success.

THE HAZARDS OF SUCCESS

The wisdom encapsulated in the notion that managing failure and success stands as one of life's greatest challenges resonates profoundly. Winners, those who continually seek the next challenge, understand the pivotal role of learning in navigating the dichotomy between success and failure. They grasp the essence of constant growth through learning and adaptation. However, a pitfall arises when individuals assume that success is an assured outcome. It is a positive attitude that becomes the bedrock supporting the confidence to adapt and prevail when circumstances spiral beyond control.

There exist discernible patterns behind the consistent setbacks experienced by certain individuals. Some seem to remain oblivious when opportunity beckons, akin to being in the backyard searching for four-leaf clovers while missing the knock of opportunity at the door. Their failure to recognize and seize opportunities stems from a lack of astuteness in learning from past mistakes. Unclear objectives cast a fog over their path, leaving not only themselves but also others uncertain about their goals. This inconsistency dilutes their pursuit, lacking the steadfastness required to navigate toward their aspirations.

Moreover, a lack of robust alliances deprives them of the necessary support when challenges arise. Overemphasis on material wealth or societal status detracts from a holistic focus on growth and learning, blurring their vision and distorting priorities. Resistance to change and an aversion to adaptability stifle their progress, leaving them unprepared to weather the storms of transformation. Their lack of resilience and inability to bounce back from setbacks further compounds their struggles. Additionally, their failure to leverage their strengths amplifies the impact of their weaknesses, rendering them more debilitating than necessary.

The overarching life lesson embedded in these observations is the cardinal importance of never taking one's attitude for granted. Winners consistently emerge victorious because they recognize the instrumental role of attitude in shaping outcomes. Attitude indeed stands as the linchpin distinguishing winners from losers. The evidence supporting this assertion permeates our daily experiences, presenting a stark choice—how one interprets and acts upon this evidence remains a personal choice, shaping the trajectory of success or failure. Ultimately, it is the proactive cultivation and nurturing of a positive and adaptive attitude that differentiates winners from losers and charts the course toward enduring success.

Do you wish for greater acceptance?
Think Positively to brighten personality.
Do you wish to be more successful?

Think Positively to develop your career.
Do you wish to have more ability?
Think Positively to improve your skills.
Do you wish to be happier?
Think Positively to improve your judgments.
Do you wish your life to be better tomorrow?
Think Positive thoughts today.

'Attitude is the scale on which we balance our strengths and limitations. Outside circumstances are less important in the long run than our inner view of our selves.'

2

INTERPRETING YOUR WORLD

'Any fact facing us is not as important as our attitude toward it, for that determines our success or failure.'

—Norman Vincent Peale

Initiating the journey towards a positive attitude necessitates a foundational step: acknowledging and comprehending the true essence of one's current attitude. However, this introspective task often proves more complex than anticipated. Yet, the way individuals react to diverse situations serves as a mirror reflecting their fundamental attitude towards life.

To thrive in any pursuit or endeavour, the bedrock remains a positive or affirmative disposition. This disposition acts as a catalyst, shaping the lens through which challenges are perceived and addressed. It serves as a guiding force, steering actions and reactions towards constructive and optimistic pathways.

Self-awareness plays a pivotal role in this transformative process. It involves delving beneath the surface, unraveling the subtle nuances embedded within one's responses to circumstances. These reactions, often instinctive, provide glimpses into the underlying attitude—whether it leans towards resilience, optimism, cynicism or defeatism.

Understanding the true nature of one's attitude requires a conscious effort to decode the underlying thought patterns, emotional reactions and behavioural cues in various scenarios. This entails self-reflection, keen observation of personal responses, and an open-minded approach to evaluating them impartially.

Furthermore, fostering a positive attitude involves a deliberate commitment to reframe perspectives, focusing on opportunities amid challenges, and embracing a proactive approach to adversity. It requires cultivating an optimistic mindset that seeks solutions rather than dwelling on problems, thereby empowering individuals to navigate obstacles with resilience and tenacity.

Moreover, nurturing a positive attitude necessitates a willingness to embrace change and adapt to evolving circumstances. It entails recognizing the immense influence of attitude in shaping outcomes, thereby instigating a conscious effort to harness positivity as a driving force for growth and success.

The journey towards developing a positive attitude unfolds through self-awareness, introspection, and a deliberate choice to perceive life through an optimistic lens. It's a transformative process that demands mindful observation, a proactive mindset, and a commitment to continual growth. Ultimately, cultivating a positive attitude isn't just an initial step but a continuous journey—one that leads to personal empowerment, resilience, and a more fulfiling life.

YOUR POSITIVE ATTITUDE QUOTIENT (PAQ)

Let's delve deeper into the process of determining your Positive Attitude Quotient (PAQ) through a set of ten probing questions designed to gauge the frequency of exhibiting positive behaviours:

The assessment of your Positive Attitude Quotient (PAQ) revolves around ten thoughtfully crafted questions, each intended to unravel the frequency of positive behaviour in your daily life. It serves as a self-reflective tool, offering insights into the patterns and consistency of your positive attitude across various scenarios.

The scoring system—1 for 'never', 2 for 'seldom', 3 for 'sometimes', 4 for 'usually', and 5 for 'almost always'—captures the spectrum of your responses to each behaviour. Honesty and self-awareness play pivotal roles in this assessment, as the accuracy of your self-evaluation impacts the overall assessment of your Positive Attitude Quotient.

As you progress through the questionnaire, consider each question thoughtfully and objectively. Reflect on instances where you've encountered similar situations and assess your typical response. Whether it's a spontaneous act of kindness, an optimistic outlook during adversity or the ability to maintain composure under stress, each behaviour warrants careful consideration based on your usual conduct.

Upon completion of the questionnaire, the cumulative sum of the scores assigned to each behaviour provides a quantitative reflection of your Positive Attitude Quotient. It's important to remember that this assessment isn't just about the final score; rather, it's a tool for self-assessment and self-awareness, aiding in the understanding of your predisposition towards positive behaviour.

This introspective exercise lays the groundwork for self-improvement and personal growth. It acts as a starting point, highlighting areas where consistent positive behaviour is evident and areas where opportunities for enhancement exist. Embracing an honest and objective approach to this evaluation fosters a deeper understanding of your Positive Attitude Quotient, enabling you to embark on a journey of self-development and fostering a more positive outlook on life.

__________ I can quickly recover from failure.
__________ I have personal goals I am working on.
__________ I keep track of my progress on goals and make the changes needed.
__________ I make up my mind slowly whether or not I will like new people I meet.
__________ I get a lot of good ideas from other people.
__________ I can find what I need to know without much help.
__________ I don't have to be reminded to do what I agree to do.
__________ I can quickly detect people who are pessimists.
__________ I enjoy listening to people's explanations, even if I don't like them personally.
__________ I am patient with people who disagree with me.
Total: __________

The significance of your total score on the PAQ serves as a gauge to assess the depth and impact of your positive attitude across various spheres of life. It encapsulates not just your individual demeanour but also its potential influence on interpersonal dynamics and professional environments.

Scoring 40 or above signifies a robust and robustly positive attitude. This strong positive disposition augments your credibility as a leader and enhances your compatibility as a colleague. Such a disposition serves as a beacon, radiating optimism and resilience, fostering an environment of trust and inspiring others to emulate this positive outlook.

A score falling between 30 and 40 indicates a normal

positive attitude. While commendable, it signifies room for further enhancement. This level of positivity serves you well and holds the potential to be a favourable influence on those around you. It lays the groundwork for positive interactions, fostering a conducive environment where optimism and constructive thinking prevail.

However, scoring between 20 and 30 signifies a somewhat unpredictable attitude. This variability can cause confusion and uncertainty within your relationships, both at home and in the workplace. This range indicates the need for a more consistent and deliberate approach toward maintaining a positive outlook, ensuring a more stable and conducive environment for growth and cooperation.

A score below 20 signals a negative attitude, inhibiting confidence in relationships and work. This range often hinders personal growth and undermines collaborative efforts. Addressing this deficit in positivity becomes imperative to foster healthier relationships and a more productive work environment.

Using the PAQ scale as a guiding tool enables introspection and highlights areas where concerted efforts toward enhancing positivity are needed. It aids in pinpointing specific aspects of attitude that require attention and improvement. By identifying these areas, individuals can embark on a targeted journey of self-improvement, nurturing a more positive attitude that transcends personal growth and positively impacts their surroundings.

ASSESS YOUR ATTITUDE TOWARD YOURSELF

The impact of one's physical well-being on the quality of life is undeniably significant. However, it is the attitude one harbours that often becomes the linchpin determining the overall quality of life. This attitude is not just an internal disposition but also manifests outwardly, influencing interactions with others and shaping the environment.

To cultivate a positive attitude towards oneself, introspection becomes essential. Asking a series of introspective questions provides a roadmap to gauge the orientation of one's attitude:

1. **Learner or Rejecter:** the inclination to acknowledge the inherent complexity of life and the willingness to continuously learn and adapt is pivotal. Are you open to recognizing that no one possesses all the answers, fostering a disposition of continuous learning and perseverance?
2. **Effort at Work:** beyond the completion of tasks, a positive attitude is reflected in the proactive effort to suggest improvements and enhance the work environment. Are you consistently striving to do your best, showcasing enthusiasm for finding better ways to accomplish tasks?
3. **Demonstration of Enthusiasm:** enthusiasm becomes a beacon, radiating positivity in words and actions. Consider the impressions you leave on others—do your actions and conversations reflect enthusiasm? Seek feedback from friends to glean a more comprehensive perspective.
4. **Willingness to Grow:** a positive attitude involves taking responsibility for personal growth and advancement. Are you proactive in preparing yourself for progress, or do you rely solely on external guidance for direction?
5. **Embracing Change:** positivity is exhibited by an open-minded approach to change, an eagerness to experiment and a willingness to entertain suggestions. Are you receptive to change and proactive in trying new approaches?
6. **Cultivating Humour and Joy:** lastly, fostering a positive attitude involves cultivating a sense of humour, refraining from taking oneself too seriously and deriving joy from

work. Do you infuse a sense of lightness and enjoyment into your endeavours?

These questions serve as a mirror, reflecting one's attitude towards oneself. They aid in identifying areas where a shift in perspective or approach might be beneficial. Embracing a positive attitude isn't just about changing oneself but also about transforming interactions and shaping a more conducive environment that fosters growth, collaboration, and fulfilment.

EVALUATE YOUR ATTITUDE TOWARD OTHER PEOPLE

'Attitude is a little thing that makes a big difference.'

—Winston Churchill

Evaluating one's consistent positive attitude towards others requires a multifaceted approach. Here are several aspects to consider when assessing this perspective:

1. **Sincere Interest:** an authentic positive attitude towards others stems from genuine interest and concern for their well-being. Are you sincerely engaged in conversations, actively discussing their needs and concerns without pretense? Sincerity in interactions cannot be feigned but resonates through genuine empathy and care.
2. **Empathetic Perspective:** fostering a positive attitude towards others involves embracing empathy. Do you endeavour to understand their viewpoints, emotions and motivations? This entails delving deeper into their feelings, comprehending why they feel a certain way and deciphering the rationale behind their actions. Being an attentive

and empathetic listener plays a pivotal role in cultivating positive relationships.

3. **Collaborative Approach:** collaboration is a cornerstone of a positive attitude towards others. Are you adept at cooperating with individuals to achieve shared objectives? A positive attitude manifests in being a team player, valuing collective goals over personal agendas and fostering an environment of mutual respect and support.

Additionally, nurturing a consistently positive attitude towards others involves aspects beyond these considerations. It encompasses actions and behaviours that create a harmonious and supportive environment:

4. **Supportive Actions:** are you proactive in offering assistance and support to those around you? A positive attitude often manifests in actions that uplift others, offer help when needed and extend a helping hand without hesitation.
5. **Encouragement and Appreciation:** positivity thrives on encouragement and appreciation. Do you actively acknowledge and commend the efforts and accomplishments of others? Cultivating a habit of recognizing and praising achievements fosters a culture of positivity and motivation.
6. **Conflict Resolution:** handling conflicts with a positive attitude is crucial. Are you adept at managing disagreements or conflicts with a constructive and solution-oriented approach? A positive attitude involves seeking resolutions that benefit all parties involved, fostering understanding and compromise.

By introspecting on these facets, individuals can gauge the depth and consistency of their positive attitude towards others.

The goal isn't just self-reflection but the cultivation of an environment where positivity permeates interactions, fostering mutual respect, empathy and collaboration for collective growth and harmony.

ATTITUDE REFLECTS POSITIVELY AND NEGATIVELY

The influence of attitude on both personal life and professional endeavours is indeed profound. Let's expand on the impact of attitude, specifically within the context of workplace safety:

A negative attitude towards workplace safety can manifest in various detrimental behaviours that jeopardize not just individual well-being but also the collective safety of the work environment. It can breed a complacent and dismissive approach, leading to:

1. **Carelessness:** a negative attitude often fosters a casual disregard for safety protocols, with phrases like 'It doesn't really matter' indicating a lack of concern for potential hazards.
2. **Ignorance:** a dismissive attitude might result in overlooking critical safety information, with the attitude of 'I didn't know that would explode', reflecting a lack of awareness or interest in safety guidelines.
3. **Fatalism:** this negative attitude manifests as a resigned acceptance of potential risks, with sentiments like 'If it happens, it happens', indicating a fatalistic approach rather than proactive risk prevention.
4. **Cynicism:** scepticism towards safety measures dismisses their importance, often belittling safety training or awareness efforts as mere 'kid's stuff', undermining their significance.

5. **Laziness:** a negative attitude may lead to neglecting safety gear or precautions, viewing them as bothersome inconveniences rather than essential safeguards, as expressed in attitudes like 'It's too much trouble.'
6. **Recklessness and Overconfidence:** a dismissive attitude can encourage risky behaviour, with phrases like 'Danger is the spice of lif' or 'I like to live on the edge' reflecting a false sense of invincibility or thrill-seeking behaviour.

In contrast, a positive attitude towards workplace safety fosters a culture of vigilance, responsibility, and proactive engagement:

1. **Planning and Diligence:** a positive attitude prompts careful planning and adherence to safety protocols, prioritizing the right procedures to ensure safety and wellbeing.
2. **Encouragement and Support:** positive attitudes promote a collaborative approach, encouraging team members to articulate safety goals and supporting each other's safety endeavours for mutual improvement.
3. **Appreciation and Gratitude:** a positive environment acknowledges contributions and suggestions, fostering a culture of appreciation, as demonstrated by phrases like 'Thanks for that suggestion.'
4. **Thoroughness and Care:** a positive outlook emphasizes doing tasks meticulously to avoid safety hazards, ensuring tasks are completed accurately the first time to prevent potential harm.
5. **Conscientiousness and Responsibility:** a positive attitude involves taking immediate action to rectify potential hazards, reflecting a conscientious attitude to prevent accidents before they occur.
6. **Alertness and Focus:** positivity encourages mindfulness

and attentiveness, concentrating on safety measures for the benefit of everyone involved.

Ultimately, a positive attitude towards workplace safety not only ensures personal safety but also cultivates a collaborative environment where collective safety and well-being are prioritized and upheld as integral components of daily operations.

Success is not solely reliant on talent and knowledge, but also heavily influenced by one's state of mind and attitude:

The road to success is indeed multifaceted, encompassing not just inherent talent or acquired knowledge but also the indispensable element of mindset and attitude. While talent and knowledge lay the foundation, it's the state of mind that acts as the catalyst, determining the actualization of one's potential. A positive mindset acts as a force multiplier, enhancing reliability, fostering respect and cultivating an environment conducive to success.

A positive state of mind inherently breeds a sense of dependability. Positivity infuses individuals with a reliable and consistent approach, enhancing their commitment and accountability. This reliability extends beyond mere execution of tasks; it reflects in the respect and consideration one shows towards others. A positive mindset inherently drives individuals to respect and acknowledge others' contributions, fostering a culture of mutual appreciation and support.

Moreover, pride in one's work and the willingness to credit others' accomplishments are inherent traits of a positive mindset. This mindset instills a sense of ownership and responsibility towards one's work, while also acknowledging the efforts and achievements of colleagues. Collaborative enthusiasm and assistance emerge naturally from a positive mindset, as individuals seek opportunities to enhance collective efficiency and share their passion with those around them.

Simple gestures, such as a smile, become powerful tools in transmitting encouragement to others. A positive demeanour resonates contagiously, uplifting the spirits of those around and creating a ripple effect of motivation and optimism. This encouragement, once shared, often finds its way back, reinforcing the positive cycle and nurturing a supportive work environment.

Recognizing the importance of one's internal landscape in shaping attitudes is crucial. The first step in evaluating and improving attitude invariably starts with introspection. Acknowledging that the biggest obstacles often stem from within fosters a proactive approach towards self-reflection and personal growth. It's this self-awareness that becomes the cornerstone in fostering a positive mindset—one that not only propels personal success but also contributes significantly to a harmonious and productive collective environment.

In essence, success transcends mere talent and knowledge; it's the amalgamation of skills, mindset and attitude. A positive state of mind acts as a catalyst, amplifying the impact of talent and knowledge, fostering respect, collaboration and motivation within oneself and among peers.

MAKE UP YOUR MIND TO BE POSITIVE

'All human beings can alter their lives
by altering their attitudes.'

—Andrew Carnegie

Discovering joy in life's simple pleasures can be a transformative approach to embracing contentment. It's about embracing gratitude for what one has while acknowledging that life is a blend of joys and sorrows. No individual has an abundance of everything, yet each person harbours unique moments of happiness and sorrow. The art lies in tilting the balance towards laughter, making it outweigh tears by savouring the little moments of joy that life presents.

Adapting to circumstances and accepting the uncertainty of the future is a pivotal aspect of leading a fulfilling life. Avoiding all risks or seeking complete protection from misfortunes is unrealistic. Acknowledging the unpredictability of life and embracing uncertainties empowers individuals to face challenges with resilience and adaptability.

The weight of other people's opinions and societal norms can often burden decision-making. Learning to disregard excessive criticism and not allowing external influences to dictate life choices is liberating. Authenticity in one's actions and decisions yields long-term fulfilment. Embracing individuality and doing what brings personal satisfaction fosters a sense of contentment and purpose.

Envy and grudges corrode the soul and hinder personal growth. Embracing a mindset devoid of jealousy and resentment creates space for positivity and growth. Avoiding toxic relationships and nurturing diverse interests broadens horizons, even if travel isn't immediately feasible. Engaging in hobbies, exploring literature or learning about new places fosters a sense of adventure and enrichment.

Regretting missed opportunities or dwelling excessively on past mistakes can hinder progress. Instead, channeling energy into learning from past experiences without dwelling on regrets paves the way for personal growth and resilience. Steering clear of unnecessary self-blame or excessive rumination prevents one from being consumed by sorrow or self-criticism.

In essence, finding contentment amid life's complexities

involves cherishing simplicity, resilience in the face of challenges, and the courage to forge one's path. It's about embracing gratitude, living authentically, nurturing positive emotions and steering clear of negative influences to lead a fulfiling life rich in happiness and purpose.

Often, individuals get entangled in the past, holding onto grudges or lingering in regretful moments. Observing those around us who dwell on past grievances can serve as a mirror, prompting reflection on the effects of such attitudes. Considering whether such attitudes breed positivity or negativity can steer our own inclinations towards healthier mindsets.

An impactful way to counteract negativity and foster contentment is to extend a helping hand to those less fortunate. Engaging in acts of kindness not only benefits others but also nurtures a sense of gratitude and purpose within oneself. Additionally, staying actively engaged in multiple pursuits serves as a shield against unhappiness. Busyness often acts as a catalyst for productivity and joy, leaving little room for negativity to seep in.

When faced with moments of self-doubt or uncertainty, it's crucial to understand that life is an ongoing journey, not merely a fixed destination. Embracing this perspective encourages acceptance of the continual flux of life's experiences. The journey towards conclusions is perpetual, marked by constant adjustments, be it in response to change, fear, failure or even success.

New experiences often bring with them a mix of excitement and risk. Adjusting to unfamiliar circumstances or different individuals demands flexibility and emotional balance. Balancing the display of emotions, particularly in professional settings, is an essential skill in adapting to novel environments. Additionally, evaluating personal routines and consciously seeking ways to break out of potential ruts contributes to personal growth and adaptability.

The concept of self-image wields a significant impact on life outcomes. How individuals perceive themselves directly influences their attitudes, actions and eventual accomplishments. Cultivating a positive self-image can serve as a catalyst for fostering a constructive attitude, leading to actions that pave the way for success and personal fulfilment.

Embracing resilience, fostering adaptability, and nurturing a positive self-image are pivotal in navigating life's complexities. Observing the effects of negative attitudes, extending kindness to others, staying engaged in activities, embracing life as a continual journey and cultivating a positive self-perception are foundational elements that contribute to a fulfiling and purposeful life journey.

The crux of confidence, garnering respect and effecting positive change hinges significantly on nurturing and upkeeping a healthy self-image. However, the unfortunate reality is that many of us fall short in this aspect due to a lack of consistent daily self-image maintenance. This shortfall often stems from a reactive approach to life rather than an assertive and proactive stance.

A helpful analogy is envisioning self-image maintenance akin to tending to a crop. Just as a farmer cannot control the weather but can influence the quality of their crop through diligent care, individuals can shape and nurture their self-worth, confidence and opportunities by focusing on what can be controlled. This shift in perspective emphasizes the importance of taking charge of actionable steps rather than dwelling on uncontrollable external factors.

The tendency to blame external circumstances, indulge in self-pity, seek revenge or fixate on past mistakes drains valuable time and energy. The key lies in acknowledging doubts and fears without letting them become impediments. However, true change doesn't merely emerge from introspection or analysis—it necessitates active measures. It's the deliberate actions taken towards improvement that catalyse genuine transformation.

Implementing change is neither simple nor effortless; it demands unwavering determination and disciplined efforts. It requires a steadfast commitment to step beyond the comfort zone and embrace discomfort, knowing that growth and progress often stem from moments of challenge and adversity.

In short, fostering a robust self-image involves a conscious and deliberate effort towards proactive action rather than reactive responses. It entails a shift in mindset—from blaming external factors to focusing on personal agency and control. By channeling energy into actionable steps, understanding and addressing doubts and fears, and embracing disciplined efforts towards self-improvement, individuals can pave the way for enduring confidence, self-worth, and positive transformations.

CHANGE THE WAY YOU FEEL ABOUT YOURSELF

'The only disability in life is a bad attitude.'

—Scott Hamilton

Altering one's self-perception is a transformative journey that can profoundly impact personal growth and well-being. Here are several empowering suggestions to initiate positive changes in self-perception:

1. **Release the Weight of the Past:** acknowledging past mistakes and letting them go is a powerful step towards personal liberation. By physically symbolizing this

release—such as writing down past liabilities and letting them burn—you actively declare your intent to no longer be burdened by past shortcomings. Learning from these experiences is pivotal, but freeing yourself from their weight is equally essential. Recognizing that dwelling on past mistakes only hinders progress reinforces the importance of moving forward.

2. **Recognize Your Value:** embracing your strengths, competencies and achievements is crucial. Crafting a realistic and affirming résumé or list of personal attributes highlights your worth. Consistently reinforcing these positive attributes through repetition and acknowledgment cements a strong self-image. Redirecting thoughts to positive aspects encourages a shift towards a more confident and empowered self-perception.
3. **Surround Yourself with Positivity:** actively seeking motivational or inspirational content nourishes the mind and soul. Exposure to positive examples, experiences and knowledge from others acts as a catalyst for personal growth. Learning from others' successes and techniques accelerates progress, providing invaluable insights while reducing the trial-and-error process.
4. **Set Clear Goals:** establishing specific, written goals is akin to activating your subconscious goal-seeking mechanism. This subconscious reinforcement aids in overcoming obstacles, as your mind tirelessly works towards achieving these set objectives. With each goal accomplished, tangible evidence of your progress bolsters your belief in your capabilities, nurturing a positive self-image.
5. **Curate Your Emotional Environment:** taking responsibility for your emotional landscape involves consciously choosing positive influences. Surrounding

yourself with supportive, uplifting individuals fosters a nurturing environment conducive to personal growth. Recognizing that your emotional environment significantly shapes your mindset emphasizes the importance of choosing associations that align with your aspirations.

Each step in this transformative process represents a conscious effort towards self-liberation and empowerment. By releasing the weight of the past, recognizing your value, seeking positive influences, setting clear objectives and curating a supportive environment, you embark on a journey that not only reshapes your self-perception but also propels you towards personal fulfilment and success.

While these initial steps might appear straightforward, their simplicity doesn't diminish their profound impact. They serve as the bedrock upon which a robust and resilient self-image can be built. These foundational steps are backed by empirical research and have demonstrated substantial results in numerous studies and personal experiences.

At their core, these steps form the groundwork for nurturing what I refer to as an internal net worth—a composite of your beliefs, values and perception of self. This internal wealth isn't quantifiable in material terms but holds immeasurable value in shaping your mindset, actions and interactions with the world.

Believing in and nurturing your strengths and core values isn't merely a surface-level exercise but a profound commitment to self-understanding and acceptance. It's about acknowledging your abilities, talents and virtues, and embracing them as the cornerstones of your identity.

Furthermore, assuming responsibility for your worthiness and capability as a proactive and accomplished individual is pivotal. Accepting this responsibility signifies a shift from a passive stance to an empowered mindset. It's recognizing that your choices, actions, and beliefs are within your control, laying the groundwork for personal accountability and growth.

This transformational journey toward fostering a positive self-image isn't solitary; its ripples extend outward, influencing those around you. When you solidify your belief in yourself, support your values, and assume responsibility for your journey, you naturally radiate this positivity. Your actions and demeanour become a source of inspiration, influencing others by example.

Indeed, these initial steps are the bedrock of a profound personal transformation. As you internalize these beliefs and values, they not only shape your own trajectory but also position you as a beacon of positivity and empowerment for others. These steps aren't just about self-improvement; they become the catalyst for a ripple effect, fostering positive change within yourself and radiating outwards, impacting the world around you.

PULL YOURSELF UP

'Those who keep trying can renew themselves.'

The pursuit of enduring success is a journey marked by incremental progress rather than swift, overnight achievements. It's akin to embarking on a climb up a ladder where each step, each rung, represents a distinct stage of growth and learning. The story of baseball legend Eddie Matthews serves as an inspiring testament to this gradual path to success.

Eddie Matthews, a prominent figure in baseball history, didn't ascend to greatness overnight. His story illustrates the invaluable lesson of starting from humble beginnings, often at the base of the ladder, and methodically progressing upward, step by step. Matthews didn't leap to fame and recognition; instead, he diligently honed his skills, faced challenges and persistently worked his way up the ladder of success.

His journey is a testament to the dedication, resilience and perseverance required to navigate the complexities of a chosen field or endeavour. Matthews didn't bypass the essential stages of growth and development; he embraced each step, accumulating experiences and refining his craft along the way.

By highlighting Matthews' trajectory, we acknowledge the significance of patience and persistence in achieving lasting success. His story underscores the essence of embracing the process, respecting the journey and understanding that true accomplishment often involves consistent effort and gradual advancement.

Matthews' narrative serves as a poignant reminder that genuine, enduring success isn't an instant destination; rather, it's the sum total of persistent effort, learning from setbacks and steadily climbing the ladder of progress, rung by rung.

Eddie Matthews' decision at the crossroads of his baseball career reveals a profound wisdom that transcends the immediate lure of a substantial signing bonus. Despite the stark contrast between the lucrative offer from the Brooklyn Dodgers and the relatively modest one from the Boston Braves, Matthews' astute judgment led him down the path less traveled.

Opting for the Braves' offer might have seemed like a financial compromise initially, but Matthews had a deeper understanding of his own capabilities and what it truly meant to attain success. His foresight and maturity at a young age allowed him to perceive the long-term value of the decision beyond the immediate financial gain.

By choosing the Braves and their minor league teams,

Matthews consciously prioritized learning and personal growth over instant gratification. He comprehended that true mastery in baseball—or any endeavour—demanded more than just monetary rewards; it required dedication, experience and a deeper immersion into the game.

The stint in the minor leagues proved instrumental for Matthews. It served as an invaluable training ground where he not only polished his skills but also imbibed critical life lessons from seasoned veterans whose careers were on the wane. His proximity to these former major league stars became an apprenticeship in itself, offering him insights beyond the game's technicalities.

By immersing himself in this environment, Matthews absorbed invaluable principles of success: the ethos of giving his best every day, maintaining humility and fostering an unyielding commitment to winning. This formative experience laid the groundwork for his future achievements in baseball and life beyond the diamond.

Matthews' decision to eschew immediate gains for long-term development epitomizes the wisdom of investing in one's growth and education. It wasn't just about playing the game; it was about comprehending the essence of success, honing character, and fostering a mindset that transcended the game's boundaries. This foundational phase in the minor leagues ultimately became the cornerstone of his illustrious career.

Eddie Matthews' career achievements stand as a testament to the wisdom and foresight behind his decision to start in the minor leagues. His remarkable record of 512 home runs, placing him in a tie with the esteemed Ernie Banks for thirteenth on the all-time career home run list, underscores his prowess on the baseball field.

Matthews' career was adorned with numerous milestones

that illuminate the depth of his talent and dedication. His incredible feat of hitting thirty or more home runs in nine consecutive seasons stands as a record—a testament to his consistent excellence. Additionally, his remarkable ability to achieve forty or more home runs four times solidifies his legacy as a prolific home run hitter. Furthermore, his participation in ten All-Star games highlights his standing among baseball's elite.

Notably, Matthews' induction into the National Baseball Hall of Fame in 1978 cemented his place among the sport's legends, recognizing his enduring impact and stellar contributions to the game.

Moreover, contemporary research from the University of Minnesota lends empirical weight to Matthews' early career trajectory. The study underscores the advantages young individuals gain from part-time employment during their formative years. It highlights the invaluable lessons learned in time management, budgeting, financial acumen, interpersonal skills and navigating work-related stress. This revelation is a testament to the long-term benefits of acquiring skills and experiences early in life.

Matthews' decision to start in the minor leagues not only laid the groundwork for his illustrious career in baseball but also aligns with modern research highlighting the advantages of early exposure to work experiences. His story resonates as a testament to the enduring benefits of learning and acquiring vital skills at a young age, providing individuals with a solid foundation and lasting 'staying power' as they navigate their professional journeys.

REWORK MISTAKES

Richard Wagner's ascent to becoming a globally renowned composer challenges the conventional notion of success being solely driven by innate talent. While Wagner exhibited a passion for theater, art, and music, his journey was far from conventional. Contrary to the image of a prodigy, he grappled with limitations: a disdain for being on stage, modest drawing abilities confined to stick figures and a slow grasp of piano playing. Yet, his determination eclipsed any perceived lack of innate talent.

At the tender age of fifteen, Wagner dared to dream of becoming a composer. Instead of relying solely on natural aptitude, he embarked on an unconventional path of relentless self-education. He delved into the depths of the library, immersing himself in a book on composition, committed its contents to memory and used it as a stepping stone towards his ambitions.

To refine his musical acumen, he sought guidance beyond the confines of traditional education. He enlisted a violinist from the Leipzig Orchestra to enlighten him on the intricacies of chords and keys. Wagner's thirst for knowledge led him to study the technical intricacies of every orchestral instrument, diligently understanding their nuances and capabilities, except for the harp. His immersion in the works of celebrated composers like Beethoven wasn't passive admiration but a quest to decipher their mastery and decipher the secrets behind capturing distinct sounds.

Wagner's methodical approach was a testament to his unyielding determination. He didn't merely rely on his innate gifts but actively sought out mentors, absorbed knowledge voraciously and dissected the works of musical luminaries to unravel the mysteries of composition.

His story serves as a compelling narrative, demonstrating that while innate talent may provide a head start, perseverance, tenacity and an insatiable hunger for learning can triumph over perceived limitations. Wagner's journey showcases the power of dedication and self-education in surmounting obstacles and crafting an enduring legacy in the world of music.

Richard Wagner's early forays into composition were met with ridicule rather than acclaim. His initial attempt at showcasing his musical creations to an audience resulted in an unexpected response: laughter. Confronted with this humbling experience, a seventeen-year-old Wagner, overcome with embarrassment, stealthily made his exit from the theater.

To decipher the flaws in his compositions, Wagner displayed an extraordinary level of humility and willingness to learn from criticism. Seeking guidance from a local church musician, he received invaluable advice. The sage counsel was clear: before venturing into uncharted territories, Wagner needed a solid foundation in the fundamentals of music composition. Embracing this guidance, he meticulously studied the works of iconic composers like Bach and Mozart, dissecting their compositions line by line. Through this painstaking process, he gradually honed his ability to construct melodious and coherent phrases.

Armed with newfound knowledge and a determination to refine his craft, Wagner was granted a second opportunity to present his work to an audience. This time, his compositions resonated with the listeners, marking a turning point in his career trajectory. This pivotal moment not only affirmed his potential but set the stage for his ascent in the realm of music.

Moreover, Wagner's openness to inspiration from unconventional sources is a testament to his innovative spirit. A telling incident highlights his remarkable adaptability and creativity: amidst the jarring noise of a neighbour hammering on tin downstairs while he was composing, instead of being deterred, Wagner found a unique way to integrate the cacophony into his music. This unconventional fusion ultimately found its place as a significant segment in his renowned opera, *Siegfried*.

Wagner's willingness to embrace criticism, coupled with his relentless pursuit of improvement and an uncanny ability to extract inspiration from the most unlikely sources, reveals the resilience and ingenuity that characterized his artistic journey. His experiences underscore the invaluable lessons in humility, adaptability and perseverance that contributed to his eventual success in the world of music.

Philip Knight, the visionary behind Nike, ardently believed that the transformative efforts required to propel his business forward held greater personal fulfilment than the day-to-day operations of a sprawling corporation. Consequently, he relinquished this mantle to another leader. Following suit, luminaries like Bill Gates and Donald Dell pursued analogous paths. Steve Jobs, albeit experiencing a setback at Apple Computer due to a delayed response, faced ousting by shareholders. However, undeterred, he staged a triumphant return, fuelled by an unwavering determination to elevate the company to unprecedented echelons, an endeavour in which he unequivocally succeeded.

Similarly, the trajectories of Bill Gates and Donald Dell underscore the notion that a shift in roles often aligns with a broader vision. Their recognition that stewardship of a company's long-term trajectory might require a fresh perspective is a testament to the significance of adaptability in leadership. By transitioning away from the daily minutiae, they enabled a fluidity of ideas and strategies that propelled their respective ventures to new heights.

Steve Jobs' narrative embodies resilience and the tenacity to reclaim a legacy. His departure from and subsequent return to Apple reflect the complexities of corporate dynamics. Jobs' comeback, propelled by an unwavering determination, epitomizes the amalgamation of innovation, leadership, and sheer willpower. His pivotal role in reshaping Apple's trajectory highlights the impact of a visionary leader who transcended setbacks to engineer unparalleled success.

These tales collectively illuminate the intricate dance between visionary leadership, strategic delegation, and the pursuit of innovation. They serve as profound illustrations of how navigating the interplay between relinquishing day-to-day operations and steering the visionary course can redefine the trajectory of iconic companies and shape industries.

LOOK FOR A BETTER WAY

The indomitable spirit of Chester Carlson serves as a powerful testament to the transformative potential of resilience in the face of adversity. His journey epitomizes how the right attitude, fortified by an unyielding determination, can transmute setbacks into catalysts for unparalleled success.

Carlson's life, marked by early responsibilities thrust upon him due to familial circumstances, sculpted a steely resolve within him. The hardships he encountered—supporting his invalid parents at a tender age, enduring their untimely passing—fostered a tenacity that propelled him forward. These adversities became the crucible in which his unwavering determination was forged.

His pursuit of education amidst these trials, culminating in a physics degree from Cal Tech, mirrored his resolute determination. The subsequent rejections from numerous firms—eighty-two in total—only served as stepping stones, fortifying his resolve. The eventual employment at Bell Labs, though brief due to a layoff in 1933, became the prelude to his transformative journey.

Refusing to succumb to despair, Carlson embarked on a

solitary endeavour, conducting experiments within the confines of his modest apartment's kitchen. Enduring excruciating pain caused by arthritis, he channeled his suffering into an unrelenting pursuit of a solution. His daily grind of manually copying drawings amplified the agony, catalysing his quest to innovate a better alternative.

In 1938, Carlson, in collaboration with Otto Kornei, birthed the first office copier, a revolutionary breakthrough. Yet, the road to recognition was fraught with rejection. Twenty companies, including industry behemoths like General Electric, RCA and IBM, initially spurned Carlson's innovation. However, the eventual acquisition of his invention by Haloid in 1946, subsequently rebranded as Xerox in 1958, attested to the colossal success borne from Carlson's unwavering perseverance.

Chester Carlson's narrative epitomizes how adversity, when met with resilience and an unwavering spirit, can serve as the crucible for innovation and monumental success. His journey remains an enduring testament to the transformative power of determination and the unwavering pursuit of one's vision, even in the face of seemingly insurmountable obstacles.

'Hoping and wishing are never enough.
Change and improvement come only when
determination sparks action.'

3

UPGRADING CAPABILITIES

'It is not because things are difficult that we do not dare, it is because we do not dare that they are difficult.'

—Seneca

The dichotomy between capability and performance resonates deeply in understanding how aptitude alone does not guarantee actual accomplishments. The pivotal bridge between competence and tangible achievement often resides within the realm of attitude—the mindset that governs the utilization and application of our skills or ideas.

Competence, rooted in the inherent ability to achieve, serves as the foundational bedrock upon which success can be built. However, this potentiality only finds fruition when coupled with the right attitude and action. The interplay between competence and performance is symbiotic; they complement each other when aligned toward achieving goals.

Yet, competence devoid of concrete results remains inert and falls short of its transformative potential. The essence lies not merely in possessing the skillset or knowledge, but in channeling it through action, driven by a proactive and determined attitude.

Attitude, in this context, becomes the linchpin that transforms competence into performance. It's the driving force that propels individuals to harness their abilities effectively, overcoming obstacles and translating potential into tangible outcomes. The mindset, determination and resilience to persevere through challenges are the catalysts that convert raw competence into meaningful achievements.

Consider the innovators and pioneers who didn't just possess knowledge or skill but embodied the tenacity and unwavering determination to apply their capabilities toward realizing groundbreaking advancements. Their success wasn't solely rooted in their expertise but in their attitude—the relentless pursuit of their goals despite setbacks or failures.

Ultimately, the fusion of competence and attitude forges the path toward impactful performance. It's the dynamic interplay between capability, determination and execution that delineates true success. Without the driving force of a proactive attitude, even the most competent individuals may falter in converting their potential into substantial achievements.

The value of competence lies not solely in its existence but in its utilization—transformed and propelled by the right attitude. The relationship between competence and performance becomes profound when imbued with the determination and vigour necessary to materialize aspirations into reality.

Competence, akin to a flourishing garden, nurtures and expands through a multitude of factors intricately interwoven within an individual's mindset, environment, and approach. The dynamic process of competency enhancement isn't just a linear trajectory but a multifaceted amalgamation of awareness, adaptability and a conducive ecosystem.

Clarity, as a cornerstone, plays a pivotal role. When individuals are cognizant of the expectations levied upon them and are equally adept at delineating their own objectives, a roadmap towards improvement is established. Knowing one's strengths and acknowledging limitations is crucial; it instigates a quest for growth, fostering a mindset of continuous learning.

Furthermore, an understanding of where to seek assistance or resources, coupled with the ability to function with minimal guidance, empowers individuals to navigate challenges autonomously. This self-sufficiency not only bolsters confidence but also cultivates a culture of problem-solving and innovation.

Self-assessment, a linchpin in this progression, facilitates a feedback loop for improvement. The capacity to gauge one's performance against personal benchmarks ensures a trajectory towards growth. The introspective evaluation fuels a perpetual cycle of refinement, honing skills and strategies for greater efficacy.

Yet, at the heart of competence's evolution lies the nexus between accomplishment and reward. A conducive environment, where meritocracy thrives, motivates individuals to strive for excellence. When the correlation between achievement and reward is palpable, it catalyses an inherent drive to excel, fostering a culture where the most accomplished individuals are duly recognized and incentivized.

In essence, competence burgeons within a supportive ecosystem that embraces clarity, self-awareness, adaptability and the symbiotic relationship between accomplishment and reward. It's a culmination of intrinsic motivation coupled with an enabling environment that fuels the growth trajectory of competency, transforming it from a static attribute into a dynamic, ever-evolving facet of an individual's arsenal.

FOSTER EMPLOYEE COMMITMENT

Fostering commitment in employees transcends mere proficiency; it's about cultivating a profound alignment between their personal motivations and the organizational vision. It hinges on creating an environment that not only recognizes competence but also inspires a deep-seated dedication to achieving shared goals.

To instill commitment, transparency and communication are foundational. Employees need a clear understanding of the organization's mission, values and objectives. When the bigger picture is vividly painted, it becomes a guiding beacon, igniting a sense of purpose and belonging among the workforce.

Empowerment plays an instrumental role. Providing autonomy and avenues for contribution empowers employees to take ownership of their roles. When their voices are heard, and their ideas are valued, a sense of agency emerges, fostering a commitment rooted in a genuine investment in the organization's success.

Recognition and appreciation form another cornerstone. Acknowledging and rewarding contributions, irrespective of scale, validates employees' efforts. This affirmation not only bolsters morale but also reinforces the link between commitment and the acknowledgment of efforts.

A nurturing environment that encourages growth and development is pivotal. Investing in employees' professional growth through training, mentorship and opportunities for advancement communicates a vested interest in their long-term success. This investment, reciprocated by a heightened commitment, forms a symbiotic relationship between individual growth and organizational prosperity.

Moreover, fostering a culture of inclusivity and belonging

enhances commitment. When employees feel valued and respected, irrespective of their role or position, it fosters a sense of camaraderie and loyalty. This cohesion translates into a collective commitment to the organization's triumphs and endeavours.

Lastly, fostering commitment thrives on leaders setting the example. Leaders who exemplify dedication, integrity and passion for the organizational mission inspire employees to follow suit. When leadership embodies the values they espouse, it sets a compelling precedent, reinforcing the nexus between commitment and success.

In essence, fostering commitment in employees extends beyond the realms of mere competency. It's about nurturing an environment that not only harnesses skills but also cultivates a shared sense of purpose, autonomy, growth, recognition, inclusivity and exemplary leadership—all integral in forging an unshakable dedication to collective success.

Embedding these established practices within organizational frameworks can significantly bolster workplace dynamics and foster a culture of productivity, innovation and cohesion. Let's expand on these points:

1. **Encouraging Minority Opinions**: actively seek diverse perspectives during decision-making processes. Encourage dissenting views to ensure a comprehensive exploration of ideas. Embrace disagreement as a catalyst for constructive dialogue, preventing groupthink and fostering a culture that values diverse viewpoints.
2. **Rewarding Innovation and Creativity**: celebrate and publicly acknowledge novel ideas and successful innovations. Champion a culture where creativity is valued, incentivizing employees to think outside the box and

contribute their unique perspectives to problem-solving endeavours.

3. **Support for Special Circumstances**: demonstrate empathy by accommodating personal challenges or conflicts within reasonable bounds. Flexibility in managing personal schedules exhibits understanding and consideration, fostering an environment that values employees' well-being.
4. **Advance Notice for Schedule Changes**: communicate changes or overtime requirements well in advance. Respect employees' time commitments outside of work, allowing them to manage their personal responsibilities effectively, which contributes to a balanced work-life equilibrium.
5. **Promote Cooperation Over Competition**: foster a collaborative ethos by rewarding teamwork and cooperative problem-solving. Discourage an overly competitive environment that may hinder collective goals. Emphasize the collective success achieved through collaborative efforts.
6. **Identify Key Individuals**: recognize and support high-performing individuals crucial to organizational success. Understand their aspirations, provide avenues for growth and offer necessary support, thereby fortifying their commitment to the organization.
7. **Exemplify Organizational Commitment**: lead by example by upholding a steadfast commitment to the organization's goals and values. Your actions serve as a model for others, shaping the organizational culture and reinforcing the principles of dedication and allegiance.

By integrating these practices, organizations can create an environment that encourages diverse thinking, values creativity, supports individual needs and fosters a collaborative culture. These efforts not only enhance productivity but also contribute to a harmonious and engaged workforce, driving organizational success.

'Human beings can alter their lives by altering their attitudes of mind.'

—William James

HOW TO DISAGREE WITHOUT BEING DISAGREEABLE

Embracing disagreement as a constructive catalyst rather than a hindrance can significantly enrich decision-making processes and spur positive outcomes within any setting. The perception of disagreement as inherently negative often stems from the connotation of conflict or discord. However, when approached with the right mindset, divergent opinions can be transformative, leading to innovative solutions and preventing catastrophic missteps.

The adage 'When two partners always agree, one of them is not necessary' encapsulates the essence of valuing dissenting viewpoints. This mindset reframes disagreement as an opportunity rather than a stumbling block. Embracing this perspective cultivates an environment where alternate perspectives are not only welcomed but celebrated.

When someone offers a differing viewpoint, it's an opportunity to expand the breadth of consideration. Recognizing that individuals bring unique experiences and insights to the table fosters a culture that values diverse perspectives. This diversity in thought often unveils blind spots or potential pitfalls that might have been overlooked, thereby averting potentially disastrous mistakes.

Rather than viewing disagreement as a confrontation, it can be reframed as an avenue for intellectual discourse. Encouraging open dialogue and creating safe spaces for dissent fosters an atmosphere where individuals feel empowered to voice their opinions without fear of repercussion. This environment not only enriches discussions but also stimulates critical thinking and problem-solving.

Moreover, leveraging disagreement to drive collaboration is paramount. Encouraging individuals to engage in healthy debates or constructive disagreements channels their energies toward seeking common ground and consensus. This process encourages individuals to arrive at a more comprehensive understanding of complex issues, leading to well-informed decisions and innovative solutions.

The transformation of controversy into positive outcomes hinges on the attitude and approach employed. Embracing disagreement as an opportunity for growth and learning reframes it from an obstacle to a catalyst for progress. It's within this space of open dialogue and respect for diverse viewpoints that organizations and individuals can harness the power of disagreement to drive positive change and achieve optimal results.

1. **Question Your Initial Impression**: acknowledge the tendency for initial reactions in disagreeable situations to be defensive or emotionally charged. Recognize that your first instinct might not represent your best self. Take a moment to reassess before reacting.
2. **Maintain Emotional Control**: when addressing personal problems or unsatisfactory performance, strive for rationality over emotionality. Keeping a level head aids in objective assessment and resolution of issues.

3. **Prioritize Listening**: allow the other person ample opportunity to express themselves without interruption. Refrain from resisting or debating immediately, as this may create barriers to communication. Instead, aim to foster understanding by listening attentively.
4. **Seek Common Ground**: focus initially on areas of agreement after hearing out the opposing viewpoint. Emphasize commonalities to establish a foundation for constructive dialogue.
5. **Embrace Honesty and Accountability**: identify and acknowledge areas where errors or mistakes might exist. Demonstrating honesty and owning up to missteps can disarm opponents and reduce defensiveness, fostering an environment conducive to resolution.
6. **Commit to Investigating Ideas**: promise a thorough examination of their ideas or concerns and genuinely follow through. This action not only shows respect for their perspective but also acknowledges the potential merit in their suggestions.
7. **Consider Delaying Immediate Action**: propose postponing action on the matter to allow ample time for contemplation and analysis. Suggest scheduling a follow-up meeting to thoroughly explore the issues raised, enabling comprehensive consideration of all facts.
8. **Prepare for Further Discussion**: before the subsequent meeting, compile and note down the most challenging questions or concerns raised. This preparation ensures readiness to address specific points, fostering a more productive discussion.

By adhering to these steps, you can navigate disagreements with a focus on constructive dialogue, empathy and an open-minded approach. This method promotes an environment conducive to resolving conflicts and fostering mutual understanding and respect.

Contemplation in the face of controversy can serve as a powerful tool for introspection and constructive resolution. Here's an exploration of some of the self-analysing tools:

1. **Seeking Truth and Understanding**: consider the possibility that the opposing viewpoint might hold some validity or truth. Evaluate whether there might be merit in their argument or perspective. By doing so, you open yourself to a broader understanding of the situation.
2. **Assessing the Nature of Reaction**: reflect on the motive behind your reaction. Evaluate whether your response aims to alleviate the problem or merely seeks to alleviate your own frustration. Consider whether your reaction will contribute to bridging the divide or widen the gap in understanding.
3. **Considering Personal Perception**: ponder the impact of your response on how others perceive you. Will your reaction elevate their estimation of your character and professionalism, or could it potentially tarnish it? Consider the long-term implications of your actions on relationships and reputation.
4. **Weighing the Outcome**: contemplate the potential outcome of the situation. Assess whether winning the argument or conflict is worth the price you might have to pay. Analyse the short-term victory against potential long-term consequences or fallout.
5. **Silence as Strategy**: evaluate the effectiveness of remaining quiet in the face of disagreement. Consider whether the disagreement might naturally dissipate over time and if your

involvement might exacerbate or de-escalate the situation.

6. **Identifying Opportunities in Difficulty**: reevaluate the challenging situation as an opportunity for personal growth or learning. Explore what lessons or insights you have already gleaned from the controversy, viewing it as a potential catalyst for self-improvement.

By engaging in this introspective process, individuals navigate controversy with a sense of mindfulness and strategic thinking. The act of self-inquiry through these questions encourages a nuanced approach to disagreements, fostering introspection, empathy and the potential for constructive resolution. This reflective approach not only aids in conflict resolution but also cultivates personal growth and maturity in handling contentious situations.

BOUNCE BACK AND WIN

'Adversity puts iron in your flesh.'

—Somerset Maugham

Brett Favre's journey in professional sports stands as a testament to resilience and the profound lessons learned from adversity. His experience with addiction to painkillers showcased a pivotal moment that defined his career and exemplified the correlation between setbacks and ultimate triumph.

Favre's struggle with Vicodin addiction, stemming from the physical toll of relentless hits on the field, epitomizes the depth of challenges athletes often face. Despite the acclaim and success, he grappled with a personal battle that threatened not just his career but also his well-being. The decision to seek rehabilitation, driven by familial and social pressures, marked a pivotal turning point—a courageous step toward healing and redemption.

His willingness to confront and overcome his addiction paralleled his unyielding determination on the field. Emerging from rehabilitation, Favre not only conquered his dependency but also embraced sobriety, showcasing his resilience and commitment to personal growth. This transformative period became a cornerstone in his life, shaping not just his career but also his character.

Favre's subsequent achievements, including three consecutive NFL Most Valuable Player awards and a record-breaking streak of 141 straight games played, underscored his unwavering resolve and indomitable spirit. His quote, 'I may get knocked down a lot…but I'll always get back up again,' epitomizes his perseverance in the face of adversity.

His story serves as a beacon of inspiration, highlighting the invaluable lessons drawn from setbacks. It underscores the significance of resilience, the strength derived from confronting challenges head-on and the profound growth that emerges from learning and rebounding from losses.

Favre's narrative transcends the realm of professional sports, encapsulating a universal truth: enduring victory often arises from the resilience cultivated through adversity. His journey symbolizes the transformative power of perseverance, determination, and the courage to rise stronger from setbacks, showcasing that true success encompasses not just accolades on the field but also the triumph of the human spirit.

Bill Mauldin's journey from a mischievous teenager to a revered cartoonist is a testament to resilience, talent, and the power of artistic expression. His early exploits as a prankster and subsequent expulsion from high school mirrored his spirited and rebellious nature, traits that would later shape his distinct voice in the world of cartooning.

Driven by a passion for drawing, Mauldin's determination to support his family led him to take a cartooning course at a tender age, showcasing his resourcefulness and initiative. He honed his craft by illustrating an array of mediums, from menus to political posters, fostering a diverse skill set and an adaptive approach to his art.

His time in the Army during World War II became a defining chapter in Mauldin's life. Through the creation of the Willie and Joe cartoons, he skillfully captured the raw and authentic experiences of soldiers, resonating deeply with his fellow servicemen. Despite facing resistance from higher-ups who sought to stifle his portrayal of the soldiers' realities, Mauldin's cartoons found resonance among the troops for their poignant accuracy.

The unwavering support of General Dwight Eisenhower, who recognized the significance of Mauldin's work despite objections from General George Patton, underscored the impact of his cartoons on capturing the essence of soldiers' lives during wartime. Mauldin's portrayal of the soldiers' struggles and camaraderie stood as a testament to the power of art in reflecting the human experience.

Mauldin's accolades, including two Pulitzer Prizes, solidify his legacy as a pioneering artist whose work transcended mere illustration to become a poignant commentary on the human condition. His profound impact and insight into the lives of soldiers earned him respect and admiration that extended far beyond the realm of cartooning.

The honour of being buried in Arlington National Cemetery with a twenty-one gun salute signifies the enduring legacy of Mauldin's contributions. His life exemplifies the profound influence of art in capturing truth, fostering empathy, and leaving an indelible mark on history. Mauldin's story stands as a testament to the transformative power of artistic expression and the enduring impact of speaking truth through creativity.

TEST NEW SKILLS

The story of Trivial Pursuit's creation by Chris Haney and Scott Abbot serves as a poignant reminder that dismissing an idea due to perceived market saturation might mean missing out on groundbreaking opportunities.

The misconception that the board game industry had reached its zenith persisted, dissuading many from venturing into it. However, Haney and Abbot defied these assumptions and channeled their determination into creating something unique, despite the initial lukewarm reception of Trivial Pursuit.

Their perseverance in refining their creation despite setbacks—initially sluggish sales due to design and cost issues—underscored their unwavering commitment to their vision. Instead of succumbing to discouragement, they diligently sought avenues to promote their game, capitalizing on every available opportunity for exposure.

Their strategic marketing tactics, such as sending Trivial Pursuit to media outlets and celebrities, exemplify their tenacity. The endorsement from Johnny Carson on The Tonight Show served as a watershed moment, catapulting the game into the public eye and igniting a skyrocketing trajectory in sales.

This anecdote vividly illustrates that initial setbacks and underwhelming responses don't necessarily indicate a lack of market demand. Rather, they can be stepping stones toward success if met with resilience, strategic thinking and unwavering determination.

Trivial Pursuit's eventual success, with a staggering twenty million games sold in the United States alone by 1984, signifies the transformative power of persistence, innovative ideas and effective marketing strategies. Haney and Abbot's story underscores the significance of believing in one's vision, persevering through challenges and leveraging unconventional methods to turn a seemingly niche idea into a colossal success. It's a testament to the potential of unexplored market niches and the rewards awaiting those who dare to challenge conventional wisdom.

> *'The gap between mediocrity and excellence is the difference measured by two things—indifference and determination.'*

DESERVE RESPECT

The relevance of emotional intelligence in leadership is a transformative concept that redefines the conventional understanding of effective leadership. While technical expertise undoubtedly holds significance, studies spanning a myriad of companies worldwide have unveiled a groundbreaking truth: the hallmark of exceptional leadership transcends mere technical prowess. Instead, it hinges significantly on qualities encapsulated within emotional intelligence, particularly compassion.

The distinction between outstanding leaders and their counterparts predominantly rests on attributes beyond technical acumen, accounting for a staggering 85 per cent of what sets them apart. Emotional intelligence emerges as the linchpin, playing a pivotal role in distinguishing exceptional leaders. It encapsulates a nuanced understanding of emotions, both personal and social, culminating in a profound impact on leadership efficacy.

'Emotional intelligence' stands as a composite of personal

and social competence, constituting the bedrock of effective leadership. Personal competence encompasses self-awareness, self-regulation' and motivation—elements that enable leaders to navigate their own emotions adeptly and manage stress in high-pressure situations.

Moreover, the social competence facet of emotional intelligence encompasses empathy and adept social skills. These qualities empower leaders to navigate complex interpersonal dynamics, foster cohesive teams and inspire trust and collaboration among their subordinates.

The significance of emotional intelligence lies in its transformative impact on workplace dynamics. Leaders possessing high emotional intelligence foster an environment conducive to innovation, engagement' and productivity. Their ability to empathize, understand and communicate effectively not only nurtures a supportive workplace culture but also enhances employee satisfaction and retention.

The recognition of emotional intelligence as the cornerstone of exceptional leadership underscores the imperative for organizations to prioritize the development of these qualities in their leaders. Investing in programs and initiatives that cultivate emotional intelligence can yield profound dividends, fostering a generation of leaders who steer organizations toward success while prioritizing empathy, compassion and holistic team dynamics.

The ascension of emotional intelligence as the defining trait of exceptional leadership heralds a paradigm shift. It champions a leadership ethos centred not only on technical proficiency but also on the transformative power of compassion, empathy and astute social acumen—a recalibration that propels organizations toward resilience, adaptability and sustainable success in an increasingly complex and interconnected world.

Individuals endowed with personal competence possess a profound self-awareness that extends far beyond mere recognition of their emotions. It encompasses the ability to delve deep into their emotional landscape, discern the nuances of their feelings and navigate them with finesse. This self-awareness transcends introspection—it entails an astute evaluation of personal strengths and limitations, fostering a profound understanding of their capabilities.

Moreover, a hallmark of high emotional intelligence within personal competence lies in the adept management of emotions. Those who excel in this domain exude a self-confidence that is not just assertive but also balanced. They exhibit a mastery in steering their emotions, enabling them to remain composed and in control even amidst challenging circumstances.

Conversely, social competence is a facet of emotional intelligence that showcases an individual's acute sensitivity to the emotional landscapes of others. This proficiency in social awareness transcends mere observation—it embodies an empathic understanding of others' emotions, needs and perspectives. It involves the ability to decipher unspoken cues, enabling individuals to navigate interpersonal dynamics adeptly.

The truly socially competent individual embodies empathy—a quality that facilitates a genuine connection with others by acknowledging and understanding their emotional states. This heightened awareness allows them to navigate relationships with finesse, fostering an environment of trust, respect and mutual understanding.

Moreover, the profound insight that pride, when morphed into arrogance, can erode relationships underscores the significance of social competence. Astute individuals recognize that an unchecked ego can drive followers away, rendering leadership ineffective. They embody humility and authenticity, recognizing that genuine leadership flourishes within a context of empathy and humility.

The synergy between personal and social competence forms the bedrock of high emotional intelligence. It encapsulates a delicate balance between self-awareness and a deep understanding of others. Leaders who embody these traits foster environments that thrive on authenticity, empathy and a genuine connection—a paradigm that transcends individual achievements, nurturing collaborative success and enduring relationships within personal and professional realms.

Successful leadership transcends technical prowess; it hinges on a sophisticated understanding of human relationships and emotions. Effective leaders are adept relationship managers, wielding their emotional intelligence as a potent tool to inspire and guide.

They embody the role of an influential motivator, fostering an environment where individuals are empowered to thrive. Their ability to uplift others stems from their innate capacity to build meaningful relationships. They create a vast network, not solely for personal gain but to forge connections that foster collaboration, trust and mutual growth. Their aptitude for teamwork and collaboration accentuates their leadership, amplifying collective achievements.

Moreover, successful leaders possess the remarkable ability to regulate their emotions, keeping destructive tendencies at bay. This emotional control is intertwined with trustworthiness and flexibility—traits that cement their credibility and adaptability. They're driven by an unyielding commitment to enhancing performance, manifesting as a readiness to act decisively, particularly in challenging circumstances.

Their optimism in the face of adversity sets them apart. They view difficulties not as insurmountable obstacles but as opportunities for growth and innovation. Their resilience and unwavering positivity become beacons of hope, rallying their teams during tumultuous times.

The foundation of their success lies in their high emotional intelligence, culminating in a leadership style steeped in respect, empathy and authenticity. Their ability to navigate the intricacies of human emotions, coupled with a vision for improvement and a readiness to adapt, positions them as transformational leaders capable of inspiring and driving change.

Evolution from being an effective leader to a successful one is intrinsically linked to one's mastery of emotional intelligence. It's a journey that entails not just technical prowess but also the art of managing relationships, regulating emotions and embodying adaptability—an amalgamation that propels leaders toward achieving impactful, lasting change.

BE A COACH

'What I need is someone who will make me do what I am capable of doing.'

—Ralph Waldo Emerson

The transformative power of coaching and training in shaping attitudes and fostering growth within teams is unparalleled. Managers, in particular, wield a pivotal role in not only influencing the present but also sculpting the future trajectory of their teams.

Embracing a coaching mindset represents a paradigm shift, propelling managers into a unique position of influence. By assuming the role of a coach, they become catalysts for instigating positive change and continuous improvement within their teams. This approach transcends traditional management—it's a dynamic process aimed at harnessing the potential of each team member, nurturing their talents and fostering a culture of ongoing development.

The essence of coaching lies in its ability to seamlessly convert affirmative attitudes into tangible on-the-job improvements. It's an iterative process, a cyclical journey that begins with setting achievable goals, progresses through diligent guidance and support and culminates in celebrating achievements. However, it doesn't stop there. Instead, it renews itself, propelling the team toward new aspirations and benchmarks, thus perpetuating a cycle of growth and evolution.

Through coaching, managers empower their teams to transcend their limitations, tapping into their latent potential. By facilitating ongoing feedback, encouragement and guidance, they create an environment conducive to learning and innovation. This iterative process not only drives individual growth but also amplifies team cohesion and performance.

Moreover, the managerial role as a coach extends beyond merely imparting knowledge; it's about fostering a growth mindset that permeates the team's ethos. It's about instilling a culture of continuous learning and improvement, where successes are celebrated and failures are viewed as learning opportunities.

Ultimately, managers who embrace coaching and training initiatives sow the seeds for both individual and collective success. Their dedication to nurturing talent and fostering a culture of perpetual growth not only enhances team performance but also shapes a future where each team member thrives, contributing their best to the collective success of the organization.

The coaching areas highlighted by Franklin C. Ashby and Arthur R. Pell in *Embracing Excellence* serve as a comprehensive roadmap for cultivating a culture of growth, collaboration and effective leadership within organizations.

1. **Management Coaching**: this entails equipping leaders to clarify assignments effectively, hold team members accountable, offer guidance and support, foster consensus and provide invaluable mentoring, trust, recognition and rewards—creating an environment conducive to productivity and growth.
2. **Empathic Listening Coaching**: coaching here focuses on refining active listening skills, emphasizing the importance of talking less and listening more, asking pertinent questions, demonstrating enthusiasm, using appropriate body language and balancing seriousness with humour to forge deeper connections and understanding.
3. **Collaboration Coaching**: encouraging the development of strong relationships within and beyond the workplace, maintaining consistency in treatment, building strategic alliances, networking, fostering a win–win mindset and encouraging interactions that foster cooperation and synergy.
4. **Conflict Resolution Coaching**: coaching in this area revolves around developing constructive approaches to handling conflicts, offering clear, non-aggressive feedback and demonstrating support and respect, fostering an environment where conflicts are managed constructively.
5. **Positive Attitudes Coaching**: coaching individuals to consider diverse perspectives with an open mind, exuding enthusiasm, focusing on solutions rather than problems and presenting opposing views with a focus on mutually beneficial outcomes—a key in cultivating a constructive and optimistic workplace culture.

6. **Self-Confidence Coaching**: encouraging individuals to take calculated risks without succumbing to fear of failure, fostering resilience and assertiveness in decision-making, contributing to a more confident and proactive team.
7. **Being Respectful Coaching**: coaching emphasizes the importance of acknowledging others' contributions, fostering genuine respect for diverse viewpoints without appearing condescending, and creating an environment where every voice is valued and respected.
8. **Strategic Leadership Coaching**: this coaching delves into the cultivation of a big-picture, long-term perspective, promoting the articulation and implementation of strategic plans and fostering innovation and forward-thinking initiatives.
9. **Establishing Priorities Coaching**: equipping leaders to manage time effectively, set achievable standards, communicate expectations clearly and ensure accountability without micromanagement—contributing to an environment of clarity and efficiency.
10. **Upward Communication Coaching**: coaching focuses on maintaining effective communication with upper management, aligning with their priorities, effectively presenting concepts and promoting the accomplishments of the entire team—a key factor in organizational alignment and success.

In essence, coaching in these diverse areas serves as a catalyst for fostering a holistic, growth-oriented workplace culture, nurturing effective communication, collaboration and leadership skills essential for organizational success and employee development.

As a coach, a manager assumes a multifaceted role that

transcends traditional supervision. Beyond merely overseeing tasks, coaching represents a dynamic process facilitating continuous learning and growth within the team.

One primary facet of managerial coaching involves assessing an employee's comprehension of newly acquired knowledge or skills. Through this process, managers ensure that the learning outcomes are effectively translated into job performance. They provide guidance, demonstrate best practices and highlight areas that warrant improvement—a testament to their commitment to fostering professional development.

Moreover, effective coaching empowers managers to tailor their guidance according to individual performance. It allows them to pinpoint specific areas that require enhancement—whether it's attitudes, skills, knowledge or innate abilities. This personalized approach fosters a nuanced evaluation, paving the way for targeted interventions aimed at bolstering employee performance and fostering a culture of continuous improvement.

Accountability is a cornerstone of effective coaching. Managers utilize this opportunity to delineate specific responsibilities for each team member, fostering a sense of ownership and commitment. By establishing clear expectations and holding individuals accountable for their roles, managers instill a sense of purpose and drive, contributing to a more cohesive and goal-oriented team dynamic.

Nevertheless, it's vital to acknowledge that both coaches and individuals under their guidance are inherently imperfect. Perfection is an elusive ideal. Instead, the focus lies in striving for continuous growth and improvement, acknowledging that learning is an ongoing journey for both parties involved.

Above all, effective coaching embodies the art of recognition. Managers, as coaches, understand the significance of acknowledging and crediting achievements. By offering commendation where it's due, they foster a culture of appreciation and motivation, nurturing a positive work environment that celebrates successes and encourages further progress.

Managerial coaching transcends mere oversight; it embodies a commitment to individual growth, fostering a culture of accountability, recognition and continuous improvement—a testament to the manager's dedication to nurturing the potential and excellence of their team.

The essence of effective coaching lies in the delicate balance between influence and authority. The most successful coaches distinguish themselves not by exerting dominance but by wielding positive attitudes that inspire and empower their team members.

Effective managers understand that authority isn't solely derived from a position of power; it's cultivated through the demonstration of expertise and experience. Their profound understanding of their team's roles and responsibilities not only commands respect but also garners a deeper level of consideration for their suggestions and recommendations.

When a manager displays a thorough grasp of an individual's job functions, it communicates a genuine investment in understanding the intricacies of the team's work. This demonstration of knowledge doesn't just impress; it serves as a catalyst for others to pay closer attention to their guidance. It encourages team members to view their suggestions not just as directives but as informed insights born out of a comprehensive understanding of the work at hand.

Moreover, the art of effective coaching transcends the traditional authoritarian approach. Instead, it hinges on the power of positive attitudes and inspiration. Coaches who lead with positivity create an environment where team members feel motivated, valued and encouraged to bring their best selves to their roles.

By fostering a positive atmosphere, these coaches cultivate a culture where individuals are not only receptive to guidance but also inspired to contribute their ideas and solutions. This approach instills a sense of ownership and commitment, prompting team members to align their efforts with the team's objectives voluntarily.

The fusion of authority and positive influence represents the hallmark of effective coaching. It's not merely about asserting authority; it's about inspiring and influencing individuals positively, fostering an environment where mutual respect, trust, and collaboration thrive. This approach doesn't just yield short-term compliance; it cultivates a culture of engagement and empowerment that fuels sustained success and growth within the team.

To ensure your coaching sessions yield substantial results, consider these essential steps as you embark on the coaching journey:

1. **Conduct Comprehensive Background Review**: delve into the employee's background reports to discern crucial evidence concerning their:
   - Progress or any perceived lack thereof in their role.
   - Specific skills they possess and areas that may need improvement.
   - Potential or existing leadership capabilities that could be harnessed.
2. **Identify Current Job Responsibilities**: establish a clear understanding of the primary job responsibilities currently entrusted to the employee. This lays the groundwork for tailored coaching and development plans.
3. **Analyse Achieved Results**: assess the outcomes and achievements derived from the employee's efforts, evaluating

the effectiveness of their actions and contributions within their role.

4. **Evaluate Training Quality and Application**: scrutinize the quality and effectiveness of the training the employee has undergone. Evaluate how effectively this training has been applied in their day-to-day responsibilities and performance.

During the Coaching Sessions:

- **Communicate the Purpose of Coaching**: clearly articulate to the employee that the primary objective of coaching is to facilitate their performance enhancement and support them in achieving their best.
- **Outline Coaching Steps and Schedule**: provide a detailed overview of the coaching process, elucidating the sequential steps and the proposed schedule to align expectations and clarify the path forward.
- **Encourage Questions and Dialogue**: foster an open and interactive environment by inviting questions and ensuring that queries raised by the employee are addressed promptly and comprehensively.
- **Define Expected Results**: clearly define the anticipated outcomes and results expected from the coaching process, ensuring mutual understanding of the desired objectives and milestones.

When addressing areas necessitating improvement, adopt these strategic approaches to drive progress:

1. **Prioritize Focus Areas**: concentrate on a select one or two key areas that require improvement at a given time. By narrowing the focus, you enable deeper and more impactful exploration of these crucial facets.
2. **Encourage Self-Reflection and Analysis**: guide

the conversation toward self-criticism by prompting introspective questions. Encourage employees to reflect on their experiences, inviting queries such as, 'What new aspects did you encounter in this scenario?' or 'What alternative choices could have yielded better outcomes, and why?'

3. **Emphasize Observational Learning**: maintain a listening stance during discussions, allowing employees ample space to express their thoughts. Active observation often yields valuable insights, providing an opportunity to grasp nuances beyond verbal communication.

Furthermore, effective coaching involves meticulous documentation and planning for future sessions, ensuring a structured and fruitful coaching process:

- **Record Insights and Agenda for Future Sessions**: document observations and key points discussed for reference. Jot down specific areas to be covered in subsequent sessions, including insights on previous results and objectives yet to be accomplished.
- **Preparation for Meetings**: provide advance notice of upcoming meetings, outlining the agenda and time allocation needed. This ensures that both coach and employee are prepared and focused during sessions.

For sustained progress and improvement, employ the following strategies through ongoing contact and engagement:

1. **Acknowledge and Encourage Progress**: acknowledge and commend any progress made by the employee, reinforcing positive efforts and achievements.
2. **Define Problems Explicitly**: clearly articulate and define any encountered problems or challenges to avoid ambiguity and facilitate targeted solutions.

3. **Address Difficulties Directly**: avoid overlooking or sidestepping difficulties; address them directly, fostering a proactive approach toward resolution.
4. **Provide Continuous Support**: offer ongoing assistance and support, emphasizing a commitment to the employee's growth and development.
5. **Establish Written Improvement Goals**: solidify commitment to improvement by setting clear, documented goals that serve as guiding beacons for progress.
6. **Identify Specific Training Needs**: pinpoint and address any specific training requirements to enhance skills and capabilities effectively.
7. **Maintain Transparency in Competitive Settings**: in competitive environments, transparently communicate individual standings in relation to others, providing a clear understanding of performance benchmarks.

By implementing these meticulous and comprehensive coaching techniques, managers can foster a culture of continuous improvement, encourage self-reflection and drive sustained progress within their teams.

Effective coaching can significantly impact employee morale and performance, fostering a sense of empowerment and engagement within the workplace. When employees receive tailored guidance and support from authoritative figures, they often exhibit a higher level of job satisfaction and motivation, as they recognize the vested interest of their leaders in their success.

An insightful case reported in Inc. Magazine sheds light on the profound impact of coaching on organizational success. Bob Metcalf's decision to found Three Com Corporation was accompanied by the recognition of his managerial limitations. Understanding the critical need for expertise in certain managerial aspects, he astutely brought in Bill Kroust, a seasoned professional, to assume responsibilities where he faced challenges.

This strategic decision was not merely about filling a position but about fostering a collaborative learning environment. Metcalf's academic background had instilled a penchant for winning arguments, whereas Kroust's expertise lay in the art of salesmanship—a skillset Metcalf desired to acquire. This partnership symbolized a mutual learning opportunity, with both individuals recognizing the value in each other's expertise.

Kroust's invaluable experience in salesmanship became a conduit for Metcalf's learning, bridging the gap in his managerial skill set. Through this coaching dynamic, Metcalf expanded his horizons, gaining insights and techniques from Kroust's sales-oriented approach. This collaborative exchange epitomized the essence of coaching—transcending hierarchical roles to facilitate mutual growth and learning.

The symbiotic coaching relationship between Kroust and Metcalf transcended a unidirectional exchange of knowledge; it represented a dynamic, reciprocal learning experience that enriched both individuals involved.

Kroust, with his seasoned expertise, imparted invaluable lessons to Metcalf, delving beyond mere managerial skills. He instilled in him the significance of meticulous planning, the art of navigating through emotional intricacies and the prowess to sidestep potentially abrasive situations—an arsenal of skills crucial for effective leadership.

However, this coaching dynamic was not one-sided. Metcalf reciprocated by imparting his own expertise to Kroust, offering guidance on public speaking, steering clear of trivial pursuits and emphasizing the cardinal virtues of principles and integrity. Metcalf's mentorship extended further, encouraging an environment where individuals were empowered to take calculated risks, fostering a culture that embraced failures as part of the learning process. Additionally, he shared the profound lesson of embracing humour and levity, teaching Kroust the invaluable skill of laughing at oneself and finding humour amidst challenging situations.

Their collaboration wasn't devoid of disagreements; however, their ability to collaborate and learn from each other's diverse perspectives strengthened their individual skill sets and enhanced the company's overall resilience and capability.

The underlying essence of their coaching relationship resonates beyond hierarchical boundaries; it embodies the inherent benefits of coaching at all organizational levels. It underscores the transformative potential of seeking and providing coaching opportunities, emphasizing that growth and development are not exclusive privileges but accessible to all within the organization.

This compelling example illuminates the pivotal role of coaching in fostering a culture of continuous learning, mutual respect, and professional development. It serves as a testament to the power of collaborative coaching dynamics in bolstering individual competencies, fortifying organizational prowess and nurturing a culture that thrives on learning and collaboration.

This example underscores the transformative power of coaching partnerships within organizations. It showcases how embracing coaching as a two-way learning process can not only bridge skill gaps but also foster an environment of mutual respect, collaboration and continuous improvement. Ultimately, it highlights how effective coaching can propel individuals and organizations toward unprecedented success by leveraging diverse skill sets and learning from each other's expertise.

4

OVERCOMING PROBLEMS TOGETHER

'Do what you can, with what you have, where you are.'

—Theodore Roosevelt

WHEN THINGS GO WRONG

Navigating change and confronting errors necessitates a strategic and empathetic approach. When adversity arises, it's crucial to approach it as an opportunity for growth rather than a moment for blame. Taking a step back and evaluating the situation with an optimistic mindset lays the foundation for constructive problem-solving.

The key lies in refraining from impulsive reactions and instead opting for a composed and methodical assessment of the situation. By calmly probing into the root causes, individuals gain deeper insights into the underlying issues, paving the way for effective solutions.

Reacting emotionally tends to compound challenges, often leading to counterproductive outcomes. Resorting to punitive measures as a form of motivation can inadvertently create an environment of fear and discourage individuals from taking ownership of their actions in the future.

A more productive approach involves fostering a culture of understanding rather than instilling guilt. Embrace the role of a supportive mentor or problem-solver, guiding employees through an explorative process to identify areas of improvement. The aim is not to evoke a sense of inadequacy but to empower individuals with the knowledge and tools necessary for enhancement.

By assuming this supportive role, leaders can facilitate a learning environment where individuals feel encouraged to acknowledge shortcomings and strive for better performance. This approach doesn't just address the immediate issue at hand; it lays the groundwork for continuous improvement and fosters a culture where mistakes are viewed as opportunities for learning and growth.

Navigating challenging situations, especially when dealing with subpar work or encountering hostile personalities, requires a delicate and strategic approach. Instead of immediately resorting to criticism, it's imperative to delve into the underlying reasons behind the performance issues without assigning blame to individuals. Collaborative efforts often entail working with a diverse range of personalities, making conflict resolution and fostering productive collaboration paramount.

To effectively navigate these scenarios, consider employing the following strategies:

1. **Offering Genuine Compliments**: acknowledging and appreciating individuals, even those exhibiting hostility or underperformance, can significantly boost their self-esteem and foster a sense of value. Genuine compliments pave the way for constructive engagement and can positively influence future interactions.
2. **Avoiding Confrontations and Arguments**: Engaging in

direct confrontations with individuals displaying hostility often exacerbates their behaviour. Instead, strive to identify common ground even in challenging circumstances. Seeking understanding and commonality can act as a de-escalating strategy, disarming hostility and opening channels for constructive dialogue.

3. **Steering Clear of Humiliation or Shaming**: Reacting with humiliation or public shaming in response to subpar work or hostile behaviour only serves to deepen resentment and exacerbate conflicts. Such approaches not only fail to address the root causes but also foster a hostile environment that impedes conflict resolution and collaboration.

The overarching aim is to approach these situations with empathy and understanding, focusing on the resolution rather than exacerbation of conflicts. By refraining from immediate criticism, offering genuine appreciation, avoiding direct confrontations and steering clear of humiliation, leaders can foster an environment conducive to constructive conflict resolution and productive collaboration. These strategies lay the groundwork for building bridges and nurturing relationships, even in the face of challenging interactions or subpar work performances.

DEALING WITH CONFLICT

Conflict, in its various forms, isn't always a harbinger of negativity; rather, it's an integral facet of human interactions that presents opportunities for growth and positive transformation. How we approach and perceive conflict significantly influences its impact and eventual outcomes. Instead of viewing conflict solely through a lens of hostility or discord, consider embracing a more nuanced perspective that encompasses the potential for constructive outcomes.

Here's a deeper exploration of this idea:

1. **Shift in Perception**: instead of perceiving conflict as inherently negative or something to be shunned, consider reframing it as a catalyst for growth. Conflict, when approached with the right mindset, can yield valuable insights, foster creativity and drive innovation. Embracing this shift in perception allows individuals to see conflict as a stepping stone rather than a stumbling block.
2. **Understanding the Nature of Conflict**: conflict isn't solely about hostility; it encompasses diverse forms of opposition and discord. It manifests as differing viewpoints, contrasting opinions or even competing ideas. Recognizing this diversity within conflict allows for a more nuanced approach in addressing and resolving it.
3. **Potential for Constructive Outcomes**: while conflict may seem unsettling, acknowledging its potential for positive outcomes is crucial. When managed effectively, conflict can lead to increased collaboration, enhanced problem-solving and improved relationships. It prompts individuals to engage in meaningful discussions, fostering mutual understanding and respect.
4. **Opportunities for Learning and Growth**: viewing conflict as an opportunity for learning and personal growth reframes it as a platform for self-reflection and development. It challenges individuals to reassess their perspectives, consider alternative viewpoints and adapt their approaches, ultimately leading to personal and professional growth.

By embracing a perspective that acknowledges the potential for constructive outcomes within conflict, individuals can navigate these encounters with a sense of openness and optimism. This approach not only transforms conflict into an opportunity for positive change but also cultivates a culture that values diverse perspectives, fosters innovation and promotes collaborative problem-solving.

For individuals aiming for efficacy in conflict resolution, employing strategies to mitigate negative repercussions is crucial. Here are some reliable principles to guide you:

1. **Face-to-Face Interaction for Clarity**: opting for in-person interactions during conflicts fosters a deeper understanding of perspectives, allowing for nuanced communication and better clarity.
2. **Express Views for Relationship Building**: openly sharing viewpoints at the onset lays the groundwork for relationship management, fostering a platform for potential resolution based on mutual understanding.
3. **Balanced Discussion Platforms**: strive to minimize status disparities among conflicting parties during discussions, ensuring an equitable platform for dialogue and decision-making.
4. **Avoiding Blame Assignment**: recognize that assigning blame seldom contributes constructively to problem-solving; instead, focus on solutions and moving forward.
5. **Address Conflicts Proactively**: address conflicts at the source level whenever possible, escalating to managerial intervention only when necessary, to avoid prolonged disputes and unnecessary involvement.
6. **Maintain Flexibility in Solutions**: postpone committing to specific solutions initially, allowing room for flexibility and exploring diverse resolution options.
7. **Establish Common Ground**: identify and emphasize areas of mutual agreement early in the conflict resolution process

to build a foundation for cooperation.

8. **Highlight Mutual Benefits**: emphasize the mutual benefits of resolving conflicts, underscoring the reasons for collaboration rather than confrontation.
9. **Neutral and Impartial Language**: utilize language that remains neutral and non-judgmental to prevent unintentional escalation of emotions during discussions.
10. **Specific Error Addressing**: when addressing errors contributing to conflicts, be specific and avoid broad, sweeping statements that may escalate tensions further.
11. **Leverage Past Successes**: build coalitions based on past successful conflict resolutions to manage future challenges effectively, utilizing proven strategies for resolution.
12. **Self-Reflection for Objectivity**: prioritize self-reflection to identify personal biases or emotions that might hinder resolution efforts. Keeping these in check ensures a more objective approach to conflict resolution.

These principles serve as a comprehensive guide for effective conflict resolution, promoting understanding, fairness, and cooperation among conflicting parties. Embracing these strategies not only mitigates negative repercussions but also fosters an environment conducive to collaborative problem-solving and constructive conflict management.

GIVING CRITICISM

Enhancing receptivity to criticism can be effectively achieved by implementing the following methods:

1. **Positive Conversation Initiation**: starting the conversation positively by seeking evaluations of accomplishments fosters an environment where individuals feel valued for their

successes. This sets the tone for constructive feedback.

2. **Discuss Unsuccessful Projects**: following discussions on achievements, it's essential to delve into unsuccessful projects or errors. Inquiring about the measures that could have prevented these mistakes promotes reflection and learning from past experiences.
3. **Offer Recommendations and Suggestions**: contributing your own recommendations or alternative strategies shows your commitment to improvement. This not only demonstrates your engagement but also encourages a collaborative environment for problem-solving.
4. **Inquire About Training or Assistance**: asking about the type of training or support needed signifies your willingness to invest in the individual's development. It acknowledges that improvement requires resources and assistance, fostering a receptive environment for feedback.
5. **Establish Specific Action Steps**: collaboratively setting specific actions to improve outcomes demonstrates a commitment to change. Establishing a clear plan with defined steps enhances accountability and provides a roadmap for progress.

Incorporating these methods into discussions about performance evaluation or feedback sessions can significantly enhance receptivity to criticism. It emphasizes a balanced approach that acknowledges achievements, addresses areas for improvement and fosters a supportive environment conducive to learning and growth. This approach transforms criticism from a negative experience into an opportunity for development and positive change.

RESPONDING TO CRITICISM

Dale Carnegie's quote encapsulates a common reaction to criticism—often seen as negative or discouraging. However, the essence of conflict resolution and criticism lies not just in the skill but in the attitude with which it's approached. Unquestionably, criticism, when approached with the right mindset, can indeed be a source of immense benefit and growth.

1. **Cultivating a Growth Mindset**: embracing criticism as an opportunity for growth is fundamental. Viewing feedback as a chance to learn, adapt and improve fosters a growth-oriented mindset, transforming criticism from a setback to a stepping stone for development.
2. **Learning from Different Perspectives**: criticism often brings alternative perspectives to light. Embracing these viewpoints allows individuals to broaden their understanding and gain insights they might not have considered otherwise. It offers an opportunity to see things from a different angle.
3. **Identifying Areas for Improvement**: constructive criticism often highlights areas where one can improve. Instead of feeling discouraged, individuals can use these pointers to pinpoint specific aspects that need attention, thereby enhancing their skills or approaches.
4. **Enhancing Self-Awareness**: criticism, when received thoughtfully, can prompt introspection. It encourages individuals to evaluate their actions, reactions and behaviours, leading to heightened self-awareness and a better understanding of their impact on others.
5. **Building Resilience and Adaptability**: handling criticism in a positive manner builds resilience. It teaches individuals to navigate challenges, adapt to varying opinions and thrive

in dynamic environments—a crucial skill in personal and professional growth.

6. **Fostering Improved Communication**: addressing criticism constructively encourages open communication. It creates an environment where feedback flows freely, enabling more transparent and effective interactions among individuals or within teams.

By embracing criticism as an opportunity for growth rather than a setback, individuals can harness its potential benefits. It becomes a catalyst for personal and professional development, fostering a culture of continuous improvement, adaptability and resilience. Integrating this perspective on criticism helps individuals navigate conflicts with a more positive and solution-oriented attitude.

CONSIDER THE SOURCE

The evaluation of criticism involves multifaceted considerations that go beyond just the content of the critique. Delving deeper into the source and context of criticism provides valuable insights that can shape a more comprehensive response:

1. **Understanding the Source's Credentials**: assessing the credentials and background of the critic offers a perspective on their knowledge and expertise in the subject matter. Recognizing their experience level and access to updated information helps gauge the credibility and relevance of the critique.
2. **Recognizing Patterns in Criticism**: comparing current criticism with past instances aids in identifying patterns. Consistent feedback from the same or different sources may highlight recurring issues, offering valuable cues for improvement or validation of existing practices.

3. **Unveiling Motives Behind Criticism**: analysing the motives behind the criticism is crucial. Understanding who stands to gain or lose from the feedback sheds light on potential biases or vested interests, allowing for a more balanced interpretation of the critique.
4. **Assessing Emotional Context**: distinguishing between reactionary outbursts and composed evaluations is essential. Criticism delivered in a calm and collected manner often carries more weight, indicating a well-thought-out perspective, while emotionally charged feedback may reflect immediate emotions rather than a thoughtful assessment.
5. **Calibrating Responses to the Critique**: tailoring responses based on the nature and context of the criticism is essential. A well-reasoned, composed critique might warrant a similarly composed and analytical response, while emotional outbursts might require a more empathetic and understanding approach.
6. **Considering Diverse Perspectives**: acknowledging that different perspectives exist allows for a more comprehensive understanding of the critique. It encourages individuals to be open to varying viewpoints, fostering a culture of inclusivity and constructive dialogue.

The way one responds to criticism, particularly in leadership roles, can significantly impact personal and organizational growth. Here's a deeper exploration:

- **Navigating Vulnerability in Leadership:** leaders, by virtue of their positions, often face increased vulnerability when criticized. Their decisions and actions are under constant scrutiny. Embracing vulnerability as a part of leadership is crucial, acknowledging that mistakes and feedback are part of the growth process.

- **Reframing Criticism as an Opportunity:** Criticism, especially in leadership roles, should be seen as an opportunity for improvement rather than a personal attack. Understanding that feedback, even if delivered harshly, can contain valuable insights for professional development, strengthens a leader's ability to navigate challenging situations.
- **Significance of Recovery and Response:** how leaders recover from accusations or criticism holds immense importance. The response to criticism often shapes the organization's culture and sets a precedent for how mistakes are handled. A composed, constructive response fosters an environment of learning and resilience.
- **Learning from Adversity:** adversity, including criticism and accusations, presents an opportunity for learning. Leaders who effectively manage such situations often emerge stronger and more resilient. It's a chance to reflect on actions, reassess decisions and refine strategies for the future.
- **Evolving Through Constructive Feedback:** embracing criticism, especially when it offers constructive feedback, contributes to a leader's growth. It encourages introspection, prompts consideration of different perspectives and enables continuous improvement in leadership approaches.
- **Setting a Tone for Organizational Culture:** a leader's response to criticism sets the tone for the organizational culture. Embracing a growth-oriented mindset in the face of criticism cultivates a culture where feedback is valued, mistakes are seen as learning opportunities, and resilience is encouraged.

By reframing criticism as an opportunity for growth, leaders can navigate vulnerability, learn from adversity and set a tone that promotes a culture of learning and improvement within their organizations. Embracing criticism as a catalyst for growth, both personally and organizationally, fosters an environment where challenges are seen as opportunities for development rather than setbacks. Resilience becomes the cornerstone—how well do you rebound from adversity? Success hinges not only on managing favourable tasks but also on tackling the arduous and unpleasant duties. Striking a balance amid these challenges becomes pivotal.

Navigating through challenges, especially when faced with criticism or conflict, demands a deliberate and composed approach.

When feeling off-balance, taking a momentary pause can work wonders. It allows for a focused analysis of the core problem. Tackling issues one at a time, without succumbing to tension or worry, optimizes energy and productivity.

Criticism holds potential for improvement across an organization. Smart managers recognize the importance of swift conflict resolution. They mend disagreements promptly, reaffirming their team's value while quelling conflicts. Embracing feedback as a universal tool for growth fosters a culture of continual improvement.

Grudges often linger due to a reluctance to make amends. Pride can impede progress, leading to stalemates. Effective managers understand the importance of open conflict resolution. They take the initiative, fostering a culture where mistakes are forgiven, acknowledging that holding grudges hinders collective growth.

Forgiveness and growth become keystones in leadership. Cultivating an environment where mistakes are learned from becomes a hallmark of effective leadership. Encouraging open communication, forgiveness and learning from missteps creates a resilient and innovative team dynamic.

In essence, a deliberate problem-solving approach, embracing criticism for improvement, swift conflict resolution, and fostering a forgiving culture are crucial facets of effective leadership. These practices optimize individual and team performance while laying the groundwork for sustained growth within an organization.

'Being defeated is often only a temporary condition.
Giving up is what makes it permanent.'

—Marilyn Vos Savant

EMBRACING CONSTRUCTIVE RESPONSES

Embracing criticism as a catalyst for growth is a tough but necessary part of personal and professional development. It's not just the content of criticism that affects us; it's often the way it's delivered that stings the most.

Optimistic individuals approach criticism with resilience, viewing it as a means to rectify errors and acquire invaluable insights. They understand that the manner in which criticism is presented greatly influences its long-term impact. While one may not have control over the delivery, they do have agency over their response.

Redirecting attention from the delivery to the lessons embedded within the critique is a transformative approach. It involves shifting focus from the discomfort of the delivery to extracting the nuggets of wisdom for improvement. Understanding that a supervisor's success is intertwined with the achievements of their team fosters a realization of shared goals.

Your success or setbacks invariably reflect on them, instilling a mutual interest in your growth and development.

By focusing on the constructive aspects of criticism, individuals can turn what might initially feel like a personal attack into an opportunity for improvement. This mindset shift allows for a more objective evaluation of feedback, separating the manner of delivery from the substance of the message. It's a conscious effort to extract value from critique, irrespective of its presentation, fostering a culture of continuous learning and personal advancement.

NAVIGATING PROBLEM RESOLUTION

'The most important thing to do in solving a problem is to begin,' aptly articulated by Frank Tyger. Unresolved problems have a profound impact on morale and productivity, often rooted in several basic reasons.

1. **Subordinates' Hesitance:** employees often hesitate to provide constructive criticism to their supervisors, fearing potential repercussions or believing their feedback won't be valued within the hierarchy. This reluctance inhibits open communication necessary for effective problem-solving.
2. **Self-Preservation Mindset:** individuals might withhold input or critiques to protect their current positions or to vie for future promotions. This self-preserving behaviour can hinder candid discussions critical for identifying and addressing organizational issues.
3. **Intimidation by Expertise:** a lack of comfort in admitting knowledge gaps, especially when faced with technical expertise, can deter open dialogue. This discomfort impedes comprehensive discussions required for robust problem-solving approaches.

4. **Urgency and Hasty Judgments:** pressing timelines or urgent situations often lead to rushed, ill-considered decisions rather than deliberate, well-thought-out strategies. Quick decisions may offer immediate relief but can result in incomplete or ineffective solutions.
5. **Personal Conflicts:** unresolved personal conflicts among team members can significantly disrupt problem-solving efforts. Tensions or disagreements can overshadow collaborative work, hampering progress towards effective solutions.
6. **Narrow Perspectives:** instances where narrow perspectives dominate discussions limit the exploration of comprehensive solutions. Focusing solely on negative aspects without considering broader organizational perspectives can impede holistic problem-solving.
7. **Negative Atmosphere:** an environment entrenched in negativity, primarily concentrating on problems rather than solutions, fosters tension and uncertainty. This atmosphere hinders progress and collaborative efforts towards resolution.

Addressing these underlying obstacles involves fostering an open and inclusive culture where feedback is welcomed irrespective of hierarchical positions. Encouraging a collaborative environment that values diverse perspectives is vital for breaking communication barriers and initiating effective problem-solving processes. Creating an atmosphere that prioritizes solution-oriented discussions rather than dwelling solely on issues fosters an environment conducive to proactive resolution and sustained growth.

'A pessimist is one who makes difficulties of his opportunities and an optimist is one who makes opportunities of his difficulties.'

—Harry S. Truman

5

MOTIVATING OTHERS

'First say to yourself what you would be; and then do what you have to do.'

—Epicetus

THE INFLUENCE OF ATTITUDE IN LEADERSHIP DYNAMICS

As a manager or supervisor, your influence extends far beyond just the execution of tasks. Your demeanour, approach and interactions shape the very culture and productivity of the team. Even before officially assuming a managerial position, your attitude and behaviour significantly impact those within your immediate circle, influencing how they perceive collaboration, leadership and collective goals. These traits become crucial cornerstones as you transition into a managerial role, as your ability to inspire and lead others is integral to your success.

Becoming a manager isn't solely about holding a title; it's about being recognized as someone who can spark excellence in others. The effectiveness of your leadership often hinges on the perception of your empathy and genuine concern for the well-being of your team. Employees are often more motivated when they feel understood, valued and supported, and these qualities are instrumental in fostering a positive work environment.

In the realm of supervision, your primary responsibility revolves around cultivating unity and a shared drive among team members to achieve common objectives. This endeavour begins with establishing meaningful connections with your colleagues. Understanding their individual strengths, weaknesses, aspirations and even personal challenges such as family dynamics or external concerns lays the groundwork for nurturing a motivated, engaged and cohesive team.

By investing time and effort into understanding your team members on a personal level, you not only build rapport but also demonstrate a genuine interest in their success and well-being. This approach paves the way for fostering a team that not only works together but also supports each other's growth and collectively strives towards achieving overarching goals. Your role as a supervisor goes beyond task delegation; it's about cultivating an environment where each individual feels empowered and motivated to contribute their best, leading to a more harmonious and productive workplace.

Developing a cohesive team goes beyond just honing job-related skills. It involves delving into the intricacies of personal aspirations, family dynamics and the individual concerns that exist beyond the realms of professional duties. Understanding and acknowledging these facets of your team members' lives demonstrate a level of empathy and consideration that goes a long way in building a strong and supportive team dynamic.

One significant aspect of nurturing this positive environment is the recognition of exceptional work and the consistent display of respect towards team members. When commendable work is promptly acknowledged and celebrated, it not only boosts morale but also reinforces a sense of trust and validation within the team. Furthermore, demonstrating respect towards each team member, regardless of their role or seniority, contributes significantly to a positive work culture. This culture of mutual respect fosters an environment where every individual feels valued, contributing to a sense of camaraderie and unity among team members.

Moreover, offering support during challenging times is crucial in solidifying the perception of your commitment to your team's success. Being there for your team when they face difficulties or hurdles not only showcases your support but also reinforces the trust they have in your leadership. This support during adversity becomes instrumental in strengthening the bond between you and your team, creating a sense of security and assurance that they have someone to rely on in challenging situations.

In essence, by acknowledging accomplishments, demonstrating respect and providing support during challenging times, you not only bolster the morale and confidence of your team but also cultivate an environment where individuals feel valued, supported and motivated to contribute their best efforts. This approach lays the foundation for a cohesive and resilient team capable of overcoming obstacles and achieving collective success.

NAVIGATING THE FIELD OF OVERACHIEVERS

High achievers are often the pillars of any organization, representing not just exceptional performance but also embodying the potential for future growth and innovation. Yet, it's a common misconception that managing high achievers requires less attention or management focus compared to those with lower performance. In reality, these high performers, while immensely skilled and productive, require strategic handling and tailored support to maintain their momentum and further their growth within the organization.

Neglecting the needs of high achievers can result in missed opportunities and potential challenges for both the individual and the organization. Here's why: high performers, driven by a continuous thirst for improvement and challenge, seek environments that foster their growth. When these individuals feel stagnant or unsupported, they might become disengaged or seek opportunities elsewhere. Their ambition and drive can sometimes lead to dissatisfaction if they feel their potential isn't being maximized or recognized within their current role.

Moreover, high achievers often operate at the forefront of innovation and progress within an organization. Ignoring their needs or failing to challenge them adequately could result in underutilizing their talents. It's crucial to channel their abilities effectively, giving them space for innovation, providing challenges that align with their aspirations and ensuring their skills are continuously sharpened.

Additionally, high achievers, while performing exceptionally, might require unique management strategies. They might benefit from personalized goals, specialized training or opportunities that allow them to lead and contribute meaningfully to the organization. Failing to provide them with the necessary attention or avenues for growth might lead to frustration or a lack of motivation, hindering their overall productivity and potential contributions.

Recognizing and strategically managing high achievers is as critical as supporting and nurturing lower performers. High performers form the backbone of innovation, growth and leadership within an organization. Therefore, understanding their needs, providing avenues for growth and recognizing their contributions are essential steps to ensure their continued success and the organization's overall advancement.

1. **Progressive Assignments and Oversight:**
    - Task high achievers with challenging assignments that stretch their capabilities without overwhelming them. Offer guidance and necessary oversight, allowing them the autonomy to innovate and excel.
    - Provide projects that align with their career aspirations, serving as stepping stones for their professional growth and advancement within the organization.
2. **Recognition and Feedback:**
    - Publicly recognize and reward outstanding performance to reinforce a culture of achievement. Acknowledge their contributions in team meetings or through internal communications to highlight their impact.
    - When providing feedback or critique, ensure it occurs in private settings. This preserves their dignity and prevents unnecessary demoralization, focusing on constructive improvement rather than public scrutiny.
3. **Temporary Promotions and Growth Opportunit**ies:
    - Consider offering temporary promotions or lateral moves to assess high achievers' capabilities in leadership or higher-level roles. This approach serves as a test run for potential future responsibilities and aids in identifying future leaders within the organization.
    - Gauge their response to novel challenges and increased responsibilities. It allows them to showcase their capabilities while offering the organization insights into their leadership potential.
4. **Fostering a Culture of Innovation:**
    - High achievers often exhibit a genuine passion for their work and a commitment to excellence. Channel this

drive by encouraging them to share innovative ideas and solutions.

- Nurture an environment where overachievers feel valued and heard, leveraging their insights and innovations to drive progress. Their contributions not only benefit the organization directly but also inspire others to strive for excellence.

5. **Continuous Skill Development:**
    - Provide opportunities for continuous skill enhancement through workshops, training programmes or mentorship initiatives. Encourage their pursuit of new skills that align with their interests and the organization's needs.
    - Offer support for personal and professional growth, fostering a culture of lifelong learning that aligns with their career aspirations.

In essence, strategic empowerment and recognition of high achievers are pivotal in harnessing their potential. By providing challenging opportunities, acknowledging their contributions, assessing their leadership capabilities and nurturing a culture of innovation, organizations can benefit immensely from the talents and drive of their top performers.

IMPROVING EFFECTIVE COMMUNICATION

Effective communication is more than the mere exchange of words; it's a synergy of attitude, technique and intent that underpins the success of interactions. It's about fostering an environment where purpose propels conversations, ensuring that dialogue transcends mere exchanges to become constructive and meaningful. At the heart of effective communication lies the emphasis on acknowledging and addressing the queries and concerns raised by others.

Consideration for the perspectives and needs of others forms the cornerstone of purpose-driven interaction. When conversations prioritize the concerns, queries and viewpoints of participants, it creates a space for inclusive dialogue. This approach cultivates an environment where each voice is valued, fostering a sense of engagement and collaboration among team members.

Additionally, effective communication is underpinned by a commitment to understanding and empathy. It's not solely about conveying information; it's about comprehending the underlying motives and emotions behind the words spoken. By fostering an atmosphere where individuals feel heard, understood and respected, conversations evolve into productive exchanges, enhancing team dynamics and problem-solving capabilities.

Effective communication hinges on attitude—an attitude of openness, empathy and receptivity towards others' perspectives. It's about employing techniques that go beyond verbal articulation, encompassing active listening, body language and adaptability in approach. When purpose-driven dialogue becomes the norm, it fuels a collaborative environment where ideas flourish, conflicts find resolution and collective goals are achieved.

To foster better collaboration among colleagues, consider the following strategies:

1. **Timely Dissemination and Accessibility:**
    - Timely sharing of crucial information enables proactive decision-making and better preparedness among colleagues.
    - Ensure accessibility by utilizing efficient communication channels or platforms, facilitating easy access to essential knowledge and updates.

2. **Audience-Centric Approach:**
    - Tailoring conversations to resonate with the perspectives and concerns of the individual being addressed builds rapport and engages them in a more meaningful manner.
    - Prioritize their understanding and comfort level with the information being discussed, focusing on their needs rather than solely on personal implications.
3. **Encouraging Open Dialogue and Inclusivity:**
    - Create an open environment that encourages diverse viewpoints and promotes constructive dialogue among colleagues.
    - Solicit opinions from various team members, fostering a sense of inclusion and making individuals feel heard and valued.
4. **Embracing Expertise and Seeking Guidance:**
    - Acknowledge personal limitations and embrace the expertise of others. Encouraging a culture where seeking guidance or clarifications from subject matter experts is welcomed can enhance problem-solving and decision-making.
    - Don't hesitate to reach out to specialists or experienced colleagues when faced with uncertainties or unfamiliar territory.
5. **Conciseness and Clarity in Communication:**
    - Advocate for concise and clear communication, ensuring that messages are easy to comprehend and devoid of unnecessary complexities.
    - Avoid verbosity or jargon that might confuse or overwhelm the listener, striving for clarity to maintain engagement and comprehension.
6. **Active Listening and Feedback:**
    - Foster active listening during conversations,

acknowledging and validating the viewpoints of others. This demonstrates respect and encourages reciprocal engagement.
- Encourage constructive feedback loops, creating an environment where individuals feel comfortable providing feedback to improve communication practices.

7. **Adaptability and Flexibility:**
   - Stay adaptable in your communication style, recognizing the diversity among team members and adjusting your approach accordingly.
   - Be open to refining communication techniques based on feedback, ensuring continuous improvement in fostering fruitful exchanges.

Effective communication is a cornerstone of successful collaborations. By emphasizing timeliness, audience-centricity, open dialogue, acknowledging expertise, clarity, active listening and adaptability, organizations can create an environment conducive to better communication and enhanced teamwork.

BECOMING A BETTER LISTENER

Effective communication extends far beyond the mere exchange of words; it encompasses the pivotal role of active and attentive listening as an indispensable cornerstone. This active listening, characterized by attentiveness and engagement, forms an essential foundation for fruitful and meaningful interactions. Here are further expansions on the steps to strengthen one's capacity for attentive listening:

1. **Clarity in Listening:** beyond just hearing words, attentive listening involves striving to understand the underlying message. It entails seeking clarification where needed,

ensuring that the essence and implications of what's being communicated are crystal clear. This clarity fosters precision in response and avoids misunderstandings.

2. **Depth in Listening:** attentive listening delves beneath the surface, aiming to capture the intricate layers and varied viewpoints within the communication. It involves a curiosity to explore diverse interpretations, creating space for rich and multifaceted exchanges. This depth allows for comprehensive understanding and nuanced responses.
3. **Empathetic Listening:** beyond understanding words, attentive listening embraces the emotions, intentions and perspectives underlying the communication. It requires an empathetic connection that acknowledges and validates the feelings and viewpoints expressed by others. This fosters trust, nurtures relationships, and creates an environment where individuals feel heard and valued.
4. **Feedback-Oriented Listening:** attentive listening doesn't stop at understanding; it actively seeks feedback to ensure alignment and clarity. It involves checking for mutual understanding by summarizing or paraphrasing the received information. This feedback loop enhances communication by confirming comprehension and validating the accuracy of the exchanged information.

By embodying these aspects of attentive listening, individuals not only enhance their communication skills but also cultivate an environment conducive to robust and meaningful exchanges. Attentive listening becomes a conduit for building connections, resolving conflicts and fostering collaborative endeavours within teams and across organizations.

Active listening transcends mere auditory reception; it mandates deliberate and sustained engagement. Frequently, external distractions disrupt focus during conversations, creating a divergence between mere hearing and comprehensive understanding. The rapidity of human thought processing often leads to premature assumptions and mental tangents during these interactions.

1. **Cultivating Mindful Presence**: active listening isn't just about hearing words—it's about being fully present. Cultivating mindfulness helps resist external distractions that often infiltrate conversations. Techniques like deep breathing or mental grounding can anchor focus amidst the chaos of surrounding stimuli.
2. **Overcoming Mental Drift**: human thoughts tend to move swiftly, often leading to premature assumptions or mental tangents during conversations. To counter this, cultivating self-awareness becomes crucial. Recognizing when the mind begins to wander allows for intentional redirection of attention back to the speaker's words.
3. **Strategies for Engagement**: active listening involves conscious efforts to engage with the speaker. Techniques such as paraphrasing what was said or summarizing key points demonstrate active involvement. This not only ensures comprehension but also reassures the speaker of being heard and understood.
4. **Utilizing Non-Verbal Communication**: beyond words, non-verbal cues play a significant role. Maintaining eye contact, nodding in agreement or using affirmative gestures solidify the connection and convey genuine interest. These non-verbal signals affirm the speaker's significance in the conversation.
5. **Effective Questioning**: the art of asking thoughtful questions without interrupting the speaker's flow is a

skillful aspect of active listening. It involves curiosity and the intention to delve deeper into the speaker's thoughts, clarifying ambiguities without disrupting their narrative.

6. **Empathy and Emotional Understanding**: understanding emotions adds layers to active listening. It's about more than just comprehending words; it's about sensing the emotional tone, empathizing with the speaker's feelings and acknowledging their perspective. This understanding deepens the connection and enriches comprehension.
7. **Adaptability and Flexibility**: active listening isn't a one-size-fits-all approach. Adapting techniques to different personalities and situations is crucial. Some individuals might prefer direct engagement, while others might require more subtle forms of validation.
8. **Continuous Practice and Feedback**: developing active listening skills is an ongoing process. Regular practice, reflection and seeking feedback can refine these skills over time. Embracing feedback allows for adjustments and improvement in one's approach to listening actively.
9. **Creating a Supportive Environment**: fostering an environment where active listening is valued encourages reciprocal behaviour. When everyone in a conversation practices active listening, it establishes a culture of mutual respect and understanding.
10. **Cognitive and Emotional Load Management**: acknowledging that active listening requires cognitive and emotional investment is important. Understanding personal thresholds for managing these loads ensures sustainable and effective listening over time.

In essence, active listening is a multifaceted skill that involves not just hearing but truly understanding and empathizing with the speaker. It requires a blend of mental focus, emotional intelligence and deliberate engagement to forge meaningful connections and enhance comprehension.

Dedicated and persistent practice stands as the cornerstone of honing one's listening skills. Consistently investing time and effort in refining this proficiency leads to a heightened ability to engage with others meaningfully. Intentionally dedicating oneself to the craft of attentive listening doesn't just refine skills but elevates them, enabling individuals to immerse themselves more deeply in interactions and glean profound insights from conversations.

The dividends reaped from this deliberate cultivation of attentive listening reverberate across multifaceted domains. In the realm of relationships, be it personal or professional, the establishment of a robust rapport hinges significantly on the ability to listen actively. Through the conscientious cultivation of this skill, individuals forge connections that resonate at a deeper level, fostering trust, understanding and empathy.

In professional arenas, the impact of enhanced listening proficiency extends even further. It becomes a catalyst for productivity, innovation and effective collaboration. By actively engaging in conversations, absorbing nuances and comprehending the subtleties of colleagues' perspectives, one becomes better equipped to navigate complexities, resolve conflicts and contribute meaningfully to collective goals. The elevated listening prowess serves as a linchpin for synergy within teams, unlocking avenues for creativity and harnessing collective intelligence.

Moreover, the dividends of investing in attentive listening aren't confined solely to interpersonal dynamics. They transcend into personal growth and self-awareness. As individuals immerse themselves more deeply in others' narratives, they concurrently develop a heightened understanding of their own thought processes and biases. This introspective journey bolsters emotional intelligence and cultivates a profound sense of self-reflection, enriching one's overall persona and contributing to a more empathetic and inclusive society.

Ultimately, the deliberate pursuit of refining listening skills not only augments the depth and quality of interactions but also serves as an investment in the fabric of relationships, professional accomplishments and personal development. Its impact ripples across spheres, creating a tapestry woven with understanding, productivity and enriched human connections.

MASTERING THE ART OF EFFECTIVE QUESTIONING

The act of questioning holds equal importance to attentive listening. The potency of a well-crafted question lies in its ability to elicit a relevant and meaningful response.

1. **Precision in Inquiry**: crafting thoughtful questions is akin to wielding a key that unlocks a treasure trove of insights. The precision in formulating queries tailored to specific contexts or individuals can unravel layers of information that might remain concealed otherwise. Each question acts as a gateway to a reservoir of knowledge, experiences and perspectives, enriching the understanding between communicators.
2. **Building Bridges of Understanding**: questions aren't merely verbal exchanges; they are bridges that connect thoughts and ideas. Well-constructed questions pave the way for a more profound and holistic comprehension of a subject matter, fostering an environment where diverse

viewpoints converge and mutual understanding blossoms.

3. **Empowering Others' Voices**: a well-posed question doesn't just extract information; it empowers individuals to share their narratives. It validates their experiences and perspectives, nurturing an inclusive space where every voice feels valued and heard. This inclusive dialogue promotes a culture of respect and appreciation for diverse viewpoints.
4. **Questioning and Empathetic Listening**: the synergy between questioning and active listening is profound. Thoughtful questions demonstrate an empathetic approach to understanding others' viewpoints. They reflect an individual's commitment not just to hearing but to comprehending the nuances of another's narrative, fostering deeper connections.
5. **Quality of Decisions and Information**: the critical link between effective decision-making and the quality of information cannot be overstated. Inaccurate or insufficient information can skew decisions, leading to suboptimal outcomes. Thoughtful questioning helps in gathering comprehensive data, which serves as the bedrock for well-informed, sound judgments.
6. **Critical Thinking and Problem Solving**: questioning isn't just about extracting information; it's a catalyst for critical thinking. It encourages individuals to explore various angles, challenge assumptions and devise innovative solutions. The process of questioning nurtures a mindset geared toward problem-solving and continuous improvement.
7. **Adaptability and Learning**: embracing the art of questioning nurtures a learning-oriented mindset. It encourages adaptability and a willingness to explore the unknown. The act of questioning becomes a continuous

learning cycle, where every answer births new questions, propelling the quest for knowledge forward.

8. **Facilitating Growth and Progress**: questions serve as stepping stones for growth, both individually and collectively. They facilitate learning, spur intellectual curiosity and fuel progress across various spheres of life, contributing to personal development and the advancement of society as a whole.

The art of questioning isn't just about seeking information; it's a conduit for fostering understanding, encouraging diverse perspectives, and propelling informed decision-making and progress. A well-crafted question possesses the potential to ignite a chain reaction of discovery and growth, influencing not just the present conversation but also shaping the trajectory of future endeavours.

'Ninety-nine per cent of failures come from people who have the habit of making excuses.'

—George Washington Carver

MASTERING THE ART OF CREATIVE CRITICISM

Mastering the art of creative criticism is a delicate balance between insight and empathy, requiring both precision and compassion in delivery. It's not merely about identifying flaws but rather about understanding the intricacies that contribute to them. Effective criticism involves meticulous observation and thoughtful analysis before articulating feedback. It necessitates the ability to offer constructive suggestions aimed at improvement while maintaining a positive and encouraging tone. The art lies in highlighting strengths alongside areas for growth, fostering an environment where individuals feel empowered rather than discouraged. Mastery in this art form involves transforming critique into a catalyst for progress, inspiring proactive change while nurturing a culture that values continuous improvement and celebrates resilience in the face of challenges.

1. **Understanding the Underlying Causes**: before expressing criticism, investing time in understanding the root cause of a performance issue is crucial. This investigative approach allows for a more informed and empathetic critique. It's about delving beyond the surface to comprehend the complexities that contribute to the situation.
2. **Constructive Suggestions for Improvement**: criticism isn't about pointing fingers; it's about fostering growth. Offering constructive suggestions aimed at improvement helps individuals see a path forward. These suggestions should be tailored to the specific situation and presented in a supportive manner, focusing on solutions rather than faults.
3. **Maintaining a Positive Disposition**: critiquing while maintaining a positive outlook is a balancing act. It involves acknowledging challenges without letting them overshadow the potential for improvement. Maintaining positivity in discussions about issues cultivates an environment where individuals feel encouraged rather than demoralized.
4. **Balancing Criticism and Proactive Solutions**: constantly highlighting problems without offering solutions can hinder progress. A proactive approach involves not just identifying issues but also actively engaging in finding solutions. Balancing critique with proactive problem-solving creates a more effective environment for growth and development.
5. **Emphasizing Positivity in Critique**: the key to effective

critique lies in emphasizing positivity throughout the process. Highlighting strengths alongside areas for improvement fosters a more balanced perspective. This approach nurtures a culture of growth and improvement rather than creating a culture of blame or negativity.

6. **Motivating Positive Actions**: transforming criticism into motivation is powerful. Encouraging individuals to take positive actions towards change empowers them to address challenges proactively. Motivation becomes a driving force for individuals to initiate positive changes in their approach and actions.
7. **Becoming a Catalyst for Change**: transitioning from merely pointing out flaws to advocating for innovative ideas and positive transformations elevates your role. It positions you as someone who doesn't dwell on problems but actively seeks solutions, thereby becoming a catalyst for constructive change.
8. **Establishing a Reputation for Positive Impact**: being known as someone who emphasizes solutions and fosters a positive environment creates a reputation for being a proactive problem-solver. This reputation paves the way for collaboration, as others perceive you as someone who contributes positively to progress.
9. **Fostering an Environment of Growth and Progress**: embracing a mindset that emphasizes solutions and positive change fosters an environment conducive to growth. It encourages a culture where challenges are seen as opportunities for improvement, nurturing progress on both individual and collective levels.

In short, effective criticism isn't solely about pointing out flaws; it's about providing constructive suggestions, emphasizing positivity and actively engaging in solutions. This approach transforms critique into a catalyst for growth, positioning individuals as proponents of positive change within their circles.

TEAMING

'The essence of a team is common commitment. Without it, the members of a group perform as individuals; with it they become a powerful unit for collective performance.'

—Arthur R. Pell

Entering a team dynamic initiates a journey filled with a diverse array of challenges, necessitating adept navigation and collaborative problem-solving. How you perceive and interact with your fellow team members doesn't just impact your personal demeanour but intricately shapes the ambiance and productivity of the collective unit.

Fostering a culture that not only upholds but actively champions innovative thinking serves as the bedrock of a thriving team. This ethos surpasses the mere generation of inventive concepts; it instills a sense of unwavering commitment essential for translating those concepts into actionable results within the organizational setting. It's about nurturing an environment where creativity is both encouraged and harnessed, transforming imaginative ideas into practical solutions that propel the team forward.

The framework of triumphant teams hinges on their direct engagement in the minutiae of day-to-day decisions, their tangible contributions resulting in visible outcomes that resonate with the team's collaborative efforts and the continual recognition of exceptional performances. Active participation in decision-making not only fosters a sense of ownership but also ensures that diverse perspectives are considered, leading to more robust and well-rounded choices. Tangible outcomes serve as the manifestation of collective endeavours, solidifying the team's impact and affirming the value of collaborative work. Moreover, acknowledging exceptional performance not only motivates individuals but also reinforces a culture of appreciation, fueling a positive feedback loop that elevates team morale and productivity.

Directing the landscape of teamwork involves not only surmounting challenges but also nurturing an environment that values innovation, active involvement, visible accomplishments and the celebration of excellence. It's about fostering a culture where each team member feels empowered to contribute, resulting in a collective synergy that propels the team towards success.

When it comes to evaluating your leadership role within a team, the process is pivotal and multifaceted. Understanding the specific traits that hold paramount importance is a foundational step in this assessment. Valuable insights derived from an extensive study encompassing over 5,000 employees have shed considerable light on their perceptions regarding what constitutes effective leadership. This study, spanning diverse industries, demographics, and organizational structures, revealed a consensus on ten qualities that are universally regarded as essential for effective team leadership. These qualities emerged as undeniable markers of successful leadership, showcasing their ability to transcend barriers such as gender, age, industry size and corporate culture. In this assessment, the aim is to delve into these critical qualities in depth, analysing and understanding their nuances to better gauge their presence in one's own leadership approach. Following a meticulous evaluation of each aspect, the use of 'S' for Strong, 'A' for Average, or 'W' for Weak becomes a tool to assess personal performance against these identified traits. Moreover, soliciting evaluations from five individuals familiar with your work, employing the same criteria, adds a comprehensive layer to this introspective process, offering varied perspectives for a more holistic self-assessment.

1. ______ Offering precise directives
2. ______ Cultivating transparent and reciprocal communication
3. ______ Willingness to mentor and uplift team members
4. ______ Dispensing fair and unbiased recognition
5. ______ Establishing ongoing checks and balances
6. ______ Strategically staffing the organization with the right personnel
7. ______ Understanding the financial implications of decisions
8. ______ Fostering innovation and embracing new concepts
9. ______ Making decisive resolutions when necessary
10. ______ Consistently maintaining high levels of integrity

When evaluating oneself against external assessments, it's evident that perceptions can vary significantly. The contrast between how one perceives themselves and how others perceive them often unravels intriguing insights. Instances abound where what might be internally regarded as adept diplomacy might, from an external standpoint, come across as a hint of patronization. Similarly, the caution exercised in decision-making, seen from one's perspective as thoroughness and prudence, might be misconstrued by others as indecisiveness, leading to divergent perceptions and potential misinterpretations.

The disparities in perception become pronounced in

instances where self-realization dawns only upon receiving explicit feedback. For instance, the realization of being perceived as abrasive might come as a surprise when confronted with pointed feedback about one's demeanour or behaviour. These disparities highlight the nuanced nature of interpersonal dynamics and the intricacies inherent in how one's actions and intentions are interpreted by others.

Addressing identified weaknesses stemming from these contrasts becomes a paramount task. For instance, understanding that a perceived sense of caution might inadvertently project indecisiveness prompts a recalibration of decision-making processes. This involves a conscious effort to balance thoroughness with timeliness, ensuring decisions are well-informed yet efficiently made.

Similarly, recognizing the potential misinterpretation of diplomatic gestures as patronizing prompts a reassessment of communication styles. This might involve refining approaches to ensure that diplomatic gestures are conveyed in a manner that resonates positively and doesn't inadvertently convey an unintended tone.

By systematically addressing these identified weaknesses, one can bridge the gap between self-perception and external assessments. This involves a process of introspection, active solicitation of feedback and a commitment to evolving and refining behaviours to align more closely with intended perceptions. Ultimately, this journey of improvement isn't just about rectifying perceived weaknesses but also about fostering a deeper understanding of how one's actions are perceived and interpreted by others, leading to more effective and harmonious interpersonal interactions.

DEVELOPING YOUR INTERPERSONAL RELATIONSHIPS

Establishing and nurturing positive relationships within a professional environment is pivotal in shaping a constructive and supportive workspace. It's a cornerstone for influencing others in a positive manner and fostering a culture of collaboration and respect. The following set of ten questions serves as a reflective tool, aiming to foster an objective self-assessment regarding your impact on the office environment. Responding candidly to these questions with a simple 'yes' or 'no' lays the foundation for an honest evaluation, setting aside any personal biases or tendencies to rationalize behaviours. This self-assessment exercise acknowledges an important reality: while we might be cognizant of the motivations and circumstances that drive our actions, others judge and perceive us solely based on these actions themselves.

Reflecting on these questions enables a deeper exploration of how our conduct and presence are perceived by colleagues. It provides an opportunity to bridge the gap between intention and perception, acknowledging that sometimes, despite our best intentions, our actions might not always convey the desired impact. Moreover, this self-assessment promotes a heightened awareness of the ripple effects our behaviours have on the overall office ambiance, team dynamics and individual relationships. It encourages a more mindful approach, inviting introspection into how our presence influences the workplace atmosphere and the people around us.

The candid responses to these questions pave the way for constructive self-reflection and subsequent action. It's an exercise in humility, recognizing that personal growth often stems from acknowledging areas for improvement. By objectively assessing our influence on the office environment, we open doors to fostering better connections, refining our communication and aligning our behaviours more closely with our intended impact. Ultimately, this self-assessment isn't just about affirming positive influence; it's about identifying areas of growth and actively working towards becoming a more positive and impactful presence in the workplace.

Do you tend to be condescendingly critical? When discussing others within the organization, do you exhibit a desire to 'straighten them out'?

Yes ______ No ______

Do you feel the need for absolute control? Is it necessary for almost everything to obtain your approval?

Yes ______ No ______

During meetings, do your comments consume a disproportionate amount of time?

Yes ______ No ______

Are you quick to launch attacks?

Yes ______ No ______

Do you hesitate to grant others the same privileges or benefits that you enjoy?

Yes ______ No ______

When conversing, do you frequently use the word 'I'?

Yes ______ No ______

Are you admired by others primarily due to your strength, capability, position or status?

Yes ______ No ______

Do people perceive you as cold and distant, despite your desire for them to like you?

Yes ______ No ______

Do you consider yourself more competent than your peers or even your boss? Does your behaviour reflect this belief?

Yes ______ No ______

Do you derive satisfaction from acquiring symbols of status and power?

Yes ______ No ______

When reflecting on the assessment results, if your responses lean towards three to five 'yes' answers, it raises a flag indicating a potential perception of your conduct as abrasive. This signifies a need for introspection and potential adjustments in your approach to interpersonal interactions. However, if the assessment reveals six or more 'yes' answers, it might indicate a more significant issue requiring immediate attention and remedial action.

Understanding the impact of your behaviour on others' morale is crucial in shaping a conducive work environment. If the assessment indicates potential issues, examining your attitude and conduct becomes a critical starting point. This self-reflection aims not just at acknowledging but also at comprehending the potential implications of one's actions and their effects on colleagues' perceptions.

Implementing changes might become imperative to rectify any discrepancies between intention and perception. Companies are increasingly recognizing the significance of these nuanced interpersonal dynamics and are thus engaging executive coaches. These professionals specialize in assisting managers and individuals in gaining insights into how they are perceived, offering guidance and strategies for improvement. This proactive approach not only acknowledges the importance of self-awareness but also underscores the value of aligning one's self-perception with how they are perceived by others. Such initiatives are pivotal in fostering better workplace dynamics and enhancing collaborative relationships.

The engagement of executive coaches represents a commitment to continuous improvement and emphasizes the acknowledgment that fostering a positive work environment requires active participation and self-reflection. It's a strategic investment in personal growth and professional development, facilitating a more harmonious and productive workplace culture. By addressing potential issues highlighted by the assessment and seeking guidance where necessary, individuals can bridge gaps in perception, refine their approach and contribute to a more positive and cohesive work environment.

IMPROVING MORALE

The elevation of morale isn't something easily granted. Instead, it thrives in an environment where individuals confidently express their career aspirations, where their training needs are met and where assertiveness is embraced. It's a partnership between managers and employees that fosters such an environment. Empowering others whenever possible becomes the catalyst for augmenting morale.

When individuals believe in their ability to instigate action, exercise control over their work and actively participate in decision-making processes, a tangible enhancement in morale becomes evident.

1. **Facilitating Career Aspirations**: elevating morale is deeply

tied to creating an environment where individuals feel empowered to articulate and pursue their career aspirations. This involves fostering open communication channels where employees confidently express their professional goals, enabling managers to align organizational opportunities with individual ambitions.

2. **Addressing Training Needs**: recognizing and addressing training needs is pivotal. It demonstrates an organizational commitment to employee growth and development, nurturing a sense of investment in their skill enhancement. Providing opportunities for learning and skill-building not only enhances competence but also contributes significantly to boosting morale.
3. **Embracing Assertiveness**: a culture that embraces assertiveness empowers individuals to voice their opinions, challenge existing norms and contribute meaningfully to discussions. When assertiveness is encouraged and respected, it fosters an environment where diverse perspectives are valued, leading to a positive impact on morale.
4. **Manager–Employee Partnership**: elevating morale is a collaborative effort between managers and employees. Managers play a pivotal role in fostering an environment conducive to morale enhancement. They act as facilitators, supporting and enabling the growth and aspirations of their team members.
5. **Empowerment as a Catalyst**: empowering individuals serves as a catalyst for morale enhancement. When employees feel empowered, they exhibit increased confidence in initiating actions, taking control of their work and actively participating in decision-making processes.
6. **Belief in Action and Control**: morale flourishes when

individuals believe in their capability to drive change and exert control over their work. Empowering employees with autonomy and decision-making authority not only enhances morale but also fosters a sense of ownership and accountability.

7. **Active Participation in Decision-Making**: involving employees in decision-making processes has a profound impact on morale. It communicates trust and respect for their expertise, leading to increased engagement, satisfaction and a stronger sense of belonging within the organization.
8. **Tangible Results of Empowerment**: when individuals feel empowered, a tangible shift in morale becomes palpable. There's a noticeable increase in enthusiasm, motivation and commitment to achieving organizational goals.
9. **Creating a Positive Work Environment**: the combination of these elements—supporting career aspirations, addressing training needs, embracing assertiveness, fostering partnership and empowerment—culminates in creating a positive work environment that significantly elevates morale.
10. **Long-Term Impact**: elevating morale isn't a short-term fix; it's a continuous process that requires ongoing commitment and effort. Sustained empowerment and support pave the way for enduring positive morale, contributing to a thriving and resilient organizational culture.

CHANGE BEFORE YOU MUST

The ability to anticipate and embrace change before it becomes an urgent necessity is a skill that presents itself as a formidable challenge. It requires a proactive mindset and an openness to transformation, both of which aren't easily cultivated. However, nurturing a positive outlook has the potential to completely reframe how one perceives and navigates through change. It's about fostering a mindset that welcomes evolution and sees it as an opportunity for growth rather than an upheaval. This shift in perspective isn't without its challenges. It demands a conscious effort to break free from comfort zones and familiar routines. Yet, embracing a positive stance serves as a powerful tool in alleviating the inherent tribulations linked with change.

By adopting a positive outlook, individuals equip themselves with resilience and adaptability in the face of change. It's about acknowledging that change is an inevitable part of life and work, and by embracing it proactively, one can mitigate the disruptive effects it often brings. This positive stance fosters an environment of readiness and flexibility, enabling individuals to respond to new circumstances with agility and innovation.

Furthermore, cultivating a positive outlook towards change nurtures a growth-oriented mindset. It encourages continuous learning, as individuals seek opportunities for development within evolving situations. It prompts exploration of new ideas, methodologies and approaches, thereby enriching one's skill set and expanding horizons. This proactive approach to change not only eases the transitional process but also positions individuals to capitalize on emerging opportunities that change often unveils.

However, embracing change positively doesn't negate the challenges or complexities that come with it. It's a process that requires patience, persistence, and a willingness to adapt. Yet, by cultivating this outlook, individuals lay the groundwork for a more constructive and empowered response to change, fostering an environment conducive to innovation, growth and success amidst evolving landscapes.

Consider these comprehensive steps:

1. **Objective Introspection and Analysis**: engage in thorough introspection, dissecting your current position with a critical eye. Trace the intricate steps that have led to your present situation. Envision potential trajectories, contemplating the outcomes if no alterations are made. This reflective process provides a deeper understanding of your current status and potential future paths, fostering clarity for strategic decision-making.
2. **Identifying Mitigation Strategies**: broaden your perspective to identify potential changes that can effectively address looming threats or hazards on the horizon. Anticipate challenges and proactively seek solutions. By foreseeing potential obstacles and devising mitigation strategies, you prepare yourself to navigate uncertainties and adapt to changing landscapes, enhancing resilience in your pursuits.
3. **Setting Ambitious Goals for Distinction**: elevate your aspirations by setting ambitious and extraordinary goals. Strive for objectives that transcend the ordinary, propelling you beyond conventional boundaries. By setting lofty benchmarks, you challenge yourself to excel and distinguish your efforts, fostering a mindset oriented towards continuous growth and achievement.
4. **Leveraging Flexibility and Strengths**: cultivate flexibility by leveraging your strengths to create a diverse array of opportunities. Recognize and capitalize on your unique abilities to forge multiple pathways open for exploration and utilization. This adaptability allows you to pivot, seize new prospects and navigate various avenues, maximizing

your potential for success in different arenas.

5. **Cultivating Adaptability in Planning**: incorporate adaptability into your planning process. Develop contingency plans that accommodate various scenarios and unforeseen changes. This foresight equips you to pivot swiftly in response to evolving circumstances, ensuring resilience and effectiveness in achieving your objectives.
6. **Embracing Continuous Learning and Growth**: foster a culture of continuous learning and growth. Embrace opportunities for skill development and acquiring new knowledge. This commitment to ongoing improvement enhances your readiness to face challenges and seize opportunities, positioning you as an agile and adaptable professional.
7. **Networking and Collaboration**: foster meaningful connections and collaborations. Engage with diverse networks, exchange ideas and seek collaborations that broaden perspectives and open doors to new opportunities. Collaborative efforts often yield innovative solutions and amplify the scope of your endeavours.
8. **Embodying Resilience and Adaptation**: embody resilience and adaptability as core attributes. Embrace change as an opportunity for growth rather than a setback. This mindset shift positions you to thrive in dynamic environments, navigating challenges with resilience and agility.

Individuals who diligently strategize and meticulously prepare tend to stand out and excel compared to their counterparts who may overlook or neglect this crucial aspect. This proactive approach involves investing time and effort in careful planning, laying a solid foundation for success. By conscientiously devising strategic plans, setting clear objectives and preparing comprehensively, these individuals create a roadmap that guides their actions and decisions toward desired outcomes.

Meticulous strategizing isn't merely about creating plans; it's a deliberate process that involves thorough analysis, foresight and the identification of potential challenges and opportunities. It enables individuals to anticipate hurdles and devise contingency plans, providing a proactive advantage when faced with unforeseen circumstances. This meticulous approach allows for adaptability and agility, enabling quick responses and adjustments when navigating complex or rapidly changing environments.

Moreover, meticulous preparation encompasses a wide spectrum of activities. It involves acquiring in-depth knowledge, honing skills and harnessing resources necessary to execute plans effectively. It involves not just preparation for known tasks but also readiness for unexpected situations, ensuring a well-rounded and resilient approach.

Individuals who invest in meticulous strategizing and preparation often exhibit greater confidence in their abilities. They approach challenges with a sense of assurance, equipped with well-thought-out plans and a comprehensive understanding of the terrain they navigate. This preparation instills a sense of readiness, enabling them to seize opportunities and navigate uncertainties with poise and resilience.

Furthermore, this approach not only enhances personal performance but also contributes to fostering a culture of preparedness within teams and organizations. It sets a precedent for thoroughness, encourages proactive thinking and cultivates a mindset geared toward continuous improvement and achievement.

To proactively avoid unwelcome surprises:

1. **Specialized Expertise Development**: dedicate time and effort to hone your expertise in your field of specialization. Continuous learning and skill enhancement are crucial in staying ahead. This involves staying updated with the latest trends, innovations and best practices within your domain.
2. **Resource Identification and Familiarization**: identify essential resources pivotal to your success and familiarize yourself with their accessibility and potential applications. This encompasses not only tangible resources but also networks, mentors and knowledge repositories.
3. **Optimizing Resource Utilization**: once identified, optimize the utilization of these resources to extract maximum benefits and outcomes. Effectively leveraging resources ensures efficiency and amplifies the impact of your efforts.
4. **Progress Monitoring Mechanism**: establish an objective and quantifiable mechanism to consistently monitor and track progress. This involves setting clear metrics, milestones and checkpoints to evaluate and adjust strategies as necessary.
5. **Pragmatic Future Outlook**: foster a pragmatic outlook on the future, relying on factual information and data-driven insights rather than subjective opinions or assumptions. This approach forms a solid foundation for strategic decision-making and planning.
6. **Effective Time Management**: exercise judicious time management strategies to maximize productivity and efficiency. Prioritize tasks, allocate time effectively and minimize distractions to optimize your workflow.
7. **Unwavering Self-Discipline**: exemplify unwavering self-discipline in your actions and approaches. This involves setting boundaries, adhering to schedules and maintaining

consistency in your efforts and behaviours.

8. **Avoiding Detrimental Influences**: distance yourself from negativity and detrimental influences that might hinder your progress. Surrounding yourself with positivity, constructive influences and a supportive network helps maintain focus and motivation towards your goals.
9. **Adaptability and Flexibility**: cultivate adaptability and flexibility in your approach. While meticulous preparation is crucial, being open to adjusting strategies based on evolving circumstances ensures resilience and agility in navigating challenges.
10. **Continuous Evaluation and Adaptation**: regularly evaluate and adapt your strategies. Embrace a continuous improvement mindset, seeking feedback and being open to refining approaches based on lessons learned and changing dynamics.

In essence, meticulous strategizing and preparation lay the groundwork for success, providing individuals with a competitive edge. It's a proactive approach that not only elevates personal performance but also shapes a mindset that values preparation, adaptability and resilience—a mindset crucial for thriving in today's dynamic and challenging environments.

In the ever-evolving terrain of professional endeavours, actively expanding your knowledge base serves as a bedrock for fortifying strategic approaches and navigating the dynamic landscapes of change. By proactively embracing these elements, you not only foster an environment conducive to positive morale but also position yourself and your endeavours for resounding success.

The continuous expansion of your knowledge base isn't merely about acquiring information; it's a proactive commitment to ongoing learning and skill enhancement. This process involves staying abreast of emerging trends, industry innovations and evolving methodologies within your field. A robust knowledge foundation empowers you to make informed decisions, adapt to new challenges, and capitalize on emerging opportunities.

Fortifying strategic approaches involves leveraging the insights gained from an expanded knowledge base. It's about applying this information to refine and enhance your strategies, ensuring they align with current trends and future trajectories. By integrating this enriched understanding into your planning and execution, you create a more resilient and forward-thinking framework that anticipates and responds adeptly to change.

Proactively embracing the dynamics of change isn't passive adaptation; it's an active engagement with evolving circumstances. It involves a mindset shift that views change as an opportunity rather than a hindrance. By embracing change proactively, you cultivate flexibility, resilience and agility in your approach. This readiness enables you not only to weather uncertainties but also to identify and leverage opportunities that arise from dynamic shifts.

By diligently broadening your knowledge base through continuous learning, reinforcing your strategic approaches with innovative methods, and actively embracing and adapting to the fluid nature of change, you can create an atmosphere that not only fosters positive morale but also strategically positions itself for remarkable success within the constantly evolving realms of professional pursuits.

LEVERAGE YOUR ABILITIES

'More failure results from indecision than wrong choices.'

When navigating a pivotal moment calling for a change in direction, individuals often encounter various catalysts prompting this shift. Whether it's personal growth reaching its peak, the allure of new opportunities or simply a weariness from routine, embracing change necessitates a strategic approach. Here are five points to consider:

1. **Embracing Obstacles and Feedback:** anticipate hurdles and actively seek feedback and criticism. Cultivating resilience in the face of challenges empowers you to find innovative solutions and navigate transitions more effectively.
2. **Managing Expectations and Dedication:** acknowledge that significant progress stemming from a fresh start takes time. Maintain dedication and focus on your long-term goals while appreciating the incremental steps toward achievement.
3. **Refusing Mediocrity:** avoid settling for roles that don't align with your potential. Seek positions that allow you to creatively blend your diverse skill set, leveraging your strengths in a harmonious manner. Strive for roles that ignite passion and purpose.
4. **Continuous Learning and Adaptability:** embrace a growth mindset by continuously expanding your knowledge base. Stay adaptable and open to change, as the landscape of opportunities evolves, requiring a flexible approach.
5. **Networking and Collaboration:** engage with diverse networks and collaborative ventures. Building connections opens doors to new perspectives, opportunities and potential partnerships that can enrich your journey through transition.

By incorporating these strategies into your approach to change, you can navigate transitions more effectively, leveraging your strengths and embracing new opportunities for growth and fulfilment.

Charles Kettering, a luminary whose achievements rival the acclaim of Thomas Edison, epitomizes the archetype of a self-made inventor and industrial tycoon. His legacy reverberates through history, marked by a prolific catalogue of over 200 patents, notably his groundbreaking invention—the electronic self-starter, now an indispensable component in contemporary automobile engines. Yet, Kettering's impact transcends this invention, encompassing pioneering contributions across multiple domains, including advancements in diesel engines, anti-knock gas formulations, home air conditioning systems and innovations in rapid-drying automotive paint.

Kettering's educational journey defied convention, challenging the traditional notions of academic attainment. He held the belief that rigid adherence to established educational norms stifled innovation, fostering a reluctance to explore unconventional methodologies. Struggling with eyestrain, Kettering ingeniously adapted, relying on classmates to read aloud, a unique approach that honed his ability to visualize concepts internally—a skill integral to his inventive process. Remarkably, his resolute positivity in the face of visual impairment became a catalyst, enabling him to maximize his creative capacities.

Some proponents argue that Kettering's unparalleled achievements stemmed not despite but because of his ocular challenges. They posit that his perseverance in overcoming these hurdles endowed him with a distinct perspective, propelling his ingenuity to unforeseen heights. Kettering's ability to transcend limitations and innovate serves as a testament to the power of determination and adaptability in fostering groundbreaking advancements, illustrating that adversity can often catalyse exceptional creativity and success.

Embracing change, harnessing individual strengths and

fostering resilience constitute a formidable triad empowering individuals to navigate transitions with unwavering determination and adaptability. Drawing inspiration from trailblazers like Charles Kettering, who adeptly transformed adversities into opportunities through their distinctive outlooks and unyielding resolve, offers invaluable guidance in maneuvering through periods of change and transformation. This amalgamation of traits and insights not only facilitates a smoother transition but also paves the way for personal growth and innovative thinking, echoing the transformative spirit of those who have blazed trails before us.

AVOID DOUBTERS

'Optimists see possibilities. Pessimists refuse to look.'

The impact of influential figures on our mindset cannot be overstated. Those who hold sway over us wield the power to shape our beliefs and attitudes. If these influencers consistently espouse a narrative of impossibility, there's a perilous risk of internalizing their scepticism. Doubters and pessimists, entrenched in their convictions of what can't be achieved, often find themselves mired in stagnation or worse, regression. To foster an environment conducive to progress and personal growth, it's crucial to distance oneself from these 'mildewed' individuals—metaphorically affected by a fungus born from prolonged darkness—if one ardently believes in the potential for improvement.

In 1920, Robert Goddard, an esteemed physics professor at Clark University in Worcester, Massachusetts, authored a groundbreaking paper that boldly envisioned humanity's potential to craft a rocket capable of voyaging to the moon. This revolutionary concept reverberated across the globe, eliciting a spectrum of reactions. While some prominent publications, notably The New York Times and the London Graphic, summarily dismissed the idea, citing the perceived impossibility of propulsion in the vacuum of space due to the absence of gravitational forces, others were more disparaging. One publication even scornfully insinuated that Goddard lacked fundamental knowledge typically acquired in high school education. Nonetheless, undeterred by the scepticism, Goddard confidently asserted, 'Every vision is a joke until the first person accomplishes it,' firmly standing by his pioneering vision despite the naysayers' scepticism.

Understanding the pressing need for propulsion fuels conducive to space exploration, Goddard delved into extensive experiments centred on the amalgamation of liquid hydrogen and liquid oxygen. The former, envisioned as the propellant, while the latter served as an innovative substitute for the oxygen typically required for combustion in a terrestrial environment.

In the seminal year of 1926, Goddard's pioneering efforts bore fruit when he meticulously constructed and successfully launched a 10-foot rocket. This groundbreaking achievement saw the rocket attain a velocity of 60 mph, maintaining airborne status for a remarkable 2.5 seconds and scaling an altitude of 41 feet. Buoyed by this significant milestone, he keenly realized the mammoth challenge ahead: for a rocket to break free from Earth's gravitational clutches, it would necessitate achieving speeds surpassing 25,000 mph.

Undeterred by the enormity of this challenge, Goddard intensified his experimentation, relocating to Roswell, New Mexico, where he conducted a series of trials deploying rockets of varying sizes—ranging from 14 to 18 feet in length. These rockets showcased incremental advancements, reaching astonishing altitudes of 2,000, 7,500, and 9,000 feet, respectively. Notably, some even exceeded the speed of sound, showcasing a revolutionary implementation of fin-stabilized steering, an innovation that would shape future rocket designs.

Amidst the tumultuous backdrop of World War II, Goddard's unparalleled technological contributions resonated deeply, playing a pivotal role in the development of rockets employed in cutting-edge aircraft. Before his passing in 1945, his relentless pursuit of innovation resulted in the acquisition of an astounding 214 patents, solidifying his unequivocal standing as a trailblazer in modern rocketry. His visionary work earned him the enduring recognition as the esteemed father of space flight, a testament to his unwavering dedication and triumph over the scepticism and cynicism that once clouded the realm of interstellar exploration.

LEAN FORWARD AND DON'T LOOK BACK

The theater of war stands as an unforgiving stage where margins for error dwindle into nothingness. Within this harrowing landscape, the realm of military command operates on a razor's edge—those leaders who falter, hesitating or second-guessing their decisions, often meet the grim fate of defeat. Here, the stakes soar to unfathomable heights, where the very essence of survival hinges upon split-second decisions that become the priceless currency of existence.

Delving into the archives of history, one unearths the sagas and stratagems of celebrated military titans, each page rife with invaluable lessons etched in the blood, sweat and toil of bygone battles. These revered leaders, from Sun Tzu to Napoleon, from Alexander the Great to Patton, furnish a treasure trove of wisdom—an invaluable repository for those yearning not merely for strategic prowess on the battlefield but seeking enlightenment in realms of personal growth and improvement.

In the epic tales of warfare, one discovers not just the chronicles of conquests and defeats, but profound insights into the very essence of leadership, resilience and the essence of human nature under extreme duress. From the art of deception to the mastery of logistics, from the alchemy of motivation to the alacrity of adaptability, these narratives weave a tapestry of lessons that transcend time and circumstance.

Within the crucible of war, moments echo with the weight of eternity, where decisions made or deferred shape the contours of history. For those willing to decipher their significance, the annals of military command burgeon with a reservoir of timeless teachings—a lexicon of wisdom that enriches not just the strategist but anyone seeking to navigate the complexities of life with purpose and sagacity.

In contemplating the illustrious figure of **Ulysses S. Grant**, one is beckoned to the profound words of President Abraham Lincoln, who extolled Grant as an irreplaceable asset, 'I cannot spare this man. He fights.' Lincoln's wit, in acknowledging Grant's penchant for imbibing, further immortalized their camaraderie as he jestingly quipped, 'Inform me of his preferred brand, so I may supply it to all my generals.' This camaraderie and humour among leaders stand as a testament to the depth of their relationship.

General William T. Sherman, himself a luminary in military strategy and logistics, acknowledged Grant's unparalleled prowess, not just in confronting the exigencies of warfare but in surmounting obstacles with unwavering resolve. Sherman acknowledged, 'In matters of strategy, logistics and the intricacies of military manoeuvering, I may claim superior knowledge compared to Grant. However, there exists one domain where Grant outshines us all—he faces challenges head-on without faltering. His unwavering persistence is unparalleled.'

Grant's legacy extends beyond tactical brilliance; it embodies the spirit of resilience, an indomitable will that defies the odds. His ability to confront adversities with steadfast determination serves as a beacon of inspiration, not merely for military tacticians but for all individuals navigating the labyrinth of life's trials and tribulations. Within Grant's unwavering perseverance lies a profound lesson—a testament to the resilience of the human spirit, embodying the unwavering commitment to surmount hurdles despite the enormity of the obstacles encountered along the way.

The legendary tale of **Hannibal's** audacious endeavour to navigate a herd of elephants through the formidable Alps en route to Rome stands as a testament to his unwavering determination and audacity. In the face of scepticism from the Romans, who deemed such a feat impossible, Hannibal remained resolute in his pursuit. His famous retort, etched in history, echoes with unyielding resolve, 'We shall discover a path or forge one.'

The incredulity surrounding Hannibal's plan only fueled his determination. He embarked on a monumental journey that transcended the boundaries of what was thought achievable. Undeterred by the daunting challenge of traversing the treacherous terrain of the Alps with an army and elephants, Hannibal's indomitable spirit spurred him onward. Through sheer perseverance and strategic ingenuity, he achieved the seemingly unimaginable, etching his name into the annals of history.

Hannibal's unwavering commitment to his vision encapsulates the essence of relentless determination. His ability to confront scepticism and adversity with unshakable resolve serves as an enduring symbol of human tenacity and the unwavering pursuit of the seemingly unattainable. In his pursuit of forging a path through the Alps, Hannibal exemplified the age-old adage that where there is a will, there is indeed a way—an inspiration not just in military conquest but as a timeless lesson in the resilience of the human spirit.

In the tumultuous theater of the Battle of Mobile Bay in August 1864, **Admiral David Farragut** stood at the helm, commanding a fleet comprising a formidable arsenal of four ironclad monitors and a contingent of 14 wooden ships. Amidst the deafening barrage of Confederate gunfire, chaos ensued as a devastating mine obliterated Farragut's flagship, causing a momentary standstill in the heat of battle. Faced with this perilous juncture, some of Farragut's officers, swayed by the specter of defeat, advocated for a strategic retreat.

Yet, Admiral Farragut, a stalwart figure amidst the tempest, embodied an unwavering resolve that defied the boundaries of conventional wisdom. Undeterred by the chaos unfolding around him, Farragut's indomitable spirit ignited within him a resolute determination to push forward against all odds. In a defining moment that etched his name in the annals of naval history, Farragut seized the rigging of his battered flagship, the USS Hartford, and in a thundering act of defiance against the adversities of war, bellowed his immortal command to his crew, 'Damn the torpedoes! Full speed ahead!'

Farragut's unwavering valor and steadfast determination encapsulate the essence of courage in the face of dire circumstances. His resounding call to forge ahead despite the imminent dangers not only galvanized his crew but also stands as an enduring testament to leadership under fire. Through this resolute act, Farragut epitomized the resilience of the human spirit, illustrating that in moments of peril, true leaders do not falter but rise above, navigating through the storms of uncertainty with unyielding determination and valor.

'Courageous people look fear in the face and say, "Bring it on!"'

When queried about his exceptional prowess in strategic planning and foresight, **Napoleon Bonaparte** divulged a profound insight into his methodology, 'My appearance of perpetual preparedness is not due to a flash of genius unveiling unforeseen solutions in moments of unexpected circumstances. Rather, it is the culmination of extensive contemplation and deliberate preparation prior to embarking on any endeavour. I invest considerable time pondering potential outcomes, meticulously forecasting what might transpire. It is through this process of deep meditation and exhaustive preparation that I navigate through circumstances, appearing seemingly prescient to others.'

Napoleon's elucidation offers a testament to the power of diligent contemplation and thorough groundwork as the bedrock of foresight and readiness in the face of uncertainty.

'You lead not by what you say, but by what you do.'

The tales of these historic leaders resonate through time, immortalizing the unwavering spirits that stood firm against insurmountable odds without the slightest tremor of hesitation. Their unwavering resolve, resolute determination and unparalleled audacity to confront challenges head-on stand as guiding beacons, illuminating the path for individuals embarking on journeys of personal or professional growth.

Embedded within these accounts lie invaluable lessons, akin

to treasures waiting to be unearthed. They offer profound insights into the essence of resilience, fortitude, and the relentless pursuit of aspirations even when confronted by daunting obstacles. The echoes of their unwavering spirits resonate not merely as historical anecdotes but as timeless parables, offering solace and guidance to those navigating the labyrinthine complexities of life.

In embracing the legacies of these indomitable figures, one discovers a wellspring of wisdom, transcending the confines of time and circumstance. Their examples serve as vivid illustrations of the human capacity for perseverance and fortitude, illustrating that even in the face of seemingly insurmountable challenges, the human spirit can rise, resolute and unyielding, to conquer the adversities that beset the path to growth and achievement.

6

CONQUERING BURNOUT AND STRESS

'Expect trouble as an inevitable part of life and when it comes, hold your head high, look it squarely in the eye and say, "I will be bigger than you. You cannot defeat me."'

—Ann Landers

Every profession inherently carries its own dose of stress. In fact, a certain level of stress is vital to keep engagement alive; it injects a sense of challenge that prevents monotony from settling in. However, it's the tipping point where stress transforms into distress that issues arise. This transition often manifests through behavioural shifts. Individuals known for their unwavering patience might suddenly exhibit signs of impatience. Normally composed individuals might display visible tension. Employees, once highly cooperative, might exhibit rebellious tendencies. Others may endure physical manifestations, expressing difficulty falling asleep or maintaining a restful night's sleep. Even after a seemingly good rest, they might persistently battle fatigue, experiencing stomach discomfort, a racing heart or frequent headaches.

While physical rest can alleviate bodily fatigue, mental fatigue often persists in the workplace. This mental drain can be particularly pronounced in roles heavily reliant on computer work. Encouraging physical exercise emerges as a viable remedy. Encourage those in computer-centric roles to engage in physical activities, perhaps suggesting a lunchtime stroll, swimming, jogging or participation in a sport post-work hours. Numerous companies are now providing exercise facilities where employees can utilize stationary bikes or weight machines during their lunch breaks. Those who adhere to a consistent exercise routine tend to exhibit lower susceptibility to mental exhaustion.

By promoting physical activity as a means to counter mental fatigue, workplaces are acknowledging the interconnectedness of physical and mental well-being. Incorporating such practices not only fosters a healthier workforce but also underscores the significance of holistic wellness in combating workplace stress.

'You cannot tailor-make the situations in life, but you can tailor-make the attitudes to fit those situations before they arise.'

—Zig Ziglar

BURNOUT

Unlike light bulbs, people don't burn out abruptly like a sudden flicker in brightness followed by an abrupt outage. Human burnout is a gradual, often imperceptible process. While some instances may result in physical breakdowns like heart attacks or ulcers, the majority are primarily psychological. The signs of burnout are subtle yet pervasive. Individuals slowly lose their zest, vitality and drive, which manifests in various ways. They find themselves disliking their job, experiencing friction with colleagues, harbouring distrust toward team leaders and harbouring a pervasive sense of dread every morning as they contemplate heading to work.

Excessive stress is a prominent trigger for burnout, but it's not the sole culprit. Frustration stemming from unfulfiled promises, overlooked expected promotions or salary increments, or the relentless pressure of making critical decisions leading to potential catastrophic outcomes can all fuel burnout. Furthermore, extended work hours or unfulfiling roles are additional contributors. Those equipped with a positive mindset often navigate these challenges more adeptly.

Identifying burnout is relatively more straightforward than finding a cure. Its markers include diminished assertiveness, a tolerance for mediocrity, waning motivation to enhance performance, declining productivity and deteriorating relationships. Implementing these suggestions serves as a proactive strategy to halt the descent into a state of stagnation and disillusionment.

TEST YOUR STRESS LEVEL

Work on this stress assessment to gauge the proximity of serious stress-related issues in your life. Take a moment to delve into these queries and assign your responses in the designated box. Employ 'SA' for Strongly Affirmative, 'A' for Affirmative, 'N' for Negative, and 'SN' for Strongly Negative.

1. ______ Are you frequently fatigued throughout the day, lacking energy?
2. ______ Do you find yourself less vocal or participative in business meetings compared to your previous engagement level?

3. ______ Are instances of forgetfulness becoming more prevalent in your daily life?
4. ______ Despite adequate sleep, do you still feel persistently tired?
5. ______ Does your mental acuity seem consistently diminished or less sharp?
6. ______ Do you often feel further behind in your tasks at the end of the day compared to the outset?
7. ______ Have you noticed a decreased level of patience in your interactions with others lately?
8. ______ Are you allocating less time toward hobbies or activities you once found enjoyable?
9. ______ Do accomplishments or achievements rarely bring you satisfaction or pleasure?
10. ______ Is your performance rarely operating at maximum capacity during your waking hours?

Award yourself ten points for a Strongly Affirmative (SA) response, seven points for an Affirmative (A) answer, three points for a Negative (N) reply and zero points for a Strongly Negative (SN) response.

Now, as you evaluate your cumulative score, consider the following ranges: a score between zero to 15 signifies a state of either complete inactivity or a well-organized life; a range of 16 to 50 indicates a lower likelihood of experiencing burnout; a score from 51 to 80 suggests a precarious position where burnout could be looming; and a score of 86 to 100 signifies an elevated risk, suggesting you might be teetering on the brink as a walking stress bomb. This assessment serves as a valuable tool to help recognize and potentially address burgeoning stress-related concerns in your life.

MANAGING STRESS

Effectively managing job-related stress requires proactive measures to mitigate its impact. While some physicians might advocate for tranquilizers or other medications, self-management of stress can be achieved through the following practices:

1. Prioritize your well-being by maintaining a healthy lifestyle. Pay attention to your diet and commit to a consistent exercise regimen to keep yourself in optimal shape.
2. Embrace relaxation techniques by engaging in structured relaxation exercises. Dedicate time for solitude to unwind and recharge.
3. Foster self-respect and nurture high self-esteem. Individuals with a robust sense of self-worth are often more resilient to external pressures.
4. Acknowledge that you cannot always please everyone, underlining the importance of setting realistic boundaries.
5. Cultivate a thirst for continuous learning. Embracing ongoing learning experiences keeps your mind alert, adaptable, and invigorated.
6. Establish a reliable support network. Surround yourself with friends and family who can provide support during challenging times.
7. Assess and accept commitments that truly align with your priorities. Politely decline tasks that may excessively drain your time and energy.
8. Foster creativity in your approach to tasks. Innovate by revisiting how you handle routine responsibilities and develop fresh, creative methods to tackle new challenges, reducing their stress-inducing impact.

9. Embrace change as an avenue for new opportunities rather than perceiving it as a threat.
10. Harness the power of positive thinking. Replace negative thought patterns with positive mental images, leveraging the proven benefits of optimistic perspectives.
11. Reassess leisure activities that add to your tension. If a hobby or leisure pursuit, such as competitive sports or high-stakes games like Tournament Bridge, exacerbates stress, consider replacing it with a genuinely relaxing alternative.
12. Grant yourself permission to lead a balanced life. Delight in activities with loved ones without feeling guilty for momentarily disengaging from work-related thoughts.

By adopting these strategies, you can proactively manage stress, fostering a more harmonious balance between professional obligations and personal well-being.

'Adopting the right attitude can convert a negative stress into a positive one.'

—Hans Selye

COPING WITH BURNOUT

Achieving recovery from burnout necessitates a candid examination of fundamental issues that often contribute to this state:

1. **Conflicting objectives:** when the aspirations of the organization and your own ambitions diverge, a sense of misalignment emerges, creating a perception that avenues for professional advancement and alignment are severely limited.

2. **Monotonous and uninspiring tasks:** an excess of routine work without room for exploration or intellectual challenge fosters a stagnant environment dominated by repetitive tasks.
3. **Insufficient responsibility and influence:** a scarcity of fresh challenges or an absence of opportunities to assume greater authority can contribute to a sense of stagnation and dissatisfaction.
4. **Shifting personal priorities:** emerging familial needs or unexpected health concerns may alter the landscape, temporarily shifting the focus from career advancement to other pressing personal obligations.
5. **Evolving educational or technical demands:** unforeseen educational or technical prerequisites can jeopardize the trajectory of high achievers unless these demands are anticipated and adequate time is allocated for their fulfilment.
6. **Undervaluation despite significant effort:** instances where consistent dedication and tackling challenging tasks don't translate into commensurate recognition, praise, compensation or promotion.

In such scenarios, taking proactive steps becomes pivotal:

1. Documenting incidents and experiences that highlight the mismatch between effort and acknowledgment.
2. Engaging in introspection, reevaluating personal goals, and aligning them with professional pursuits.
3. Initiating a meeting with relevant stakeholders to address and discuss concerns surrounding the perceived lack of acknowledgment. Proactively taking charge of this conversation can potentially catalyse personal and professional growth, rather than passively waiting for external initiatives.

RELIEVING STRESS AT THE OFFICE

Alleviating stress in the office is a deeply personal journey as different approaches resonate uniquely with individuals. What proves effective for one might not necessarily yield the same results for another. However, there exist several strategies that can significantly contribute to a more balanced workday:

Taking a Timeout

Charley, when feeling the weight of undue pressure, implements a brief respite strategy. Stepping away from his desk, donning his coat and exiting the building, he takes a short ten-minute walk around the block or the parking lot. This breather helps renew his vigour and grants him a refreshed perspective.

Similarly, Esther, situated in the downtown area, chooses to escape the stress by temporarily leaving the building. Her reprieve involves a calming session of window shopping in a nearby mall.

Contrarily, Stan, restricted by a boss who disapproves of leaving during work hours, opts for a change of environment within the building. By engaging in errands in different departments, he effectively redirects his mind and eases the mounting tension.

Incorporating Exercise

While doing jumping jacks might not be ideal in a room full of colleagues, subtle exercises like controlled breathing can be discreetly performed. Inhaling deeply through the nose and exhaling slowly through the mouth for several repetitions offers a calming effect, inducing relaxation throughout the body.

Ted, benefiting from a well-equipped company gym, utilizes a short stint on a stationary bike during high-stress moments, effectively alleviating tension without breaking a sweat.

Task Rotation

When pressure surges on a particular project, shifting focus to another task for a brief interval can provide respite. Heather, overwhelmed by an impending deadline, recognized her dwindling concentration. She temporarily set aside the pressing project, diverting her attention to a different assignment for half an hour. Returning to her primary task, her mind had cleared, allowing for a renewed approach.

Seeking Companionship

For some, confiding in a friend serves as a potent stress-relief mechanism. Peter opts to discuss his stress with a close friend, acknowledging that while he doesn't expect a solution, verbalizing his thoughts to someone else helps clarify his perspective. Furthermore, casual conversation often alleviates tension in mere moments.

Find Your Own Solution

When it comes to relieving tension, a myriad of approaches can prove effective. Take, for instance, the story of an individual who, when overwhelmed with stress, retreats to the confines of his car, meticulously closing the windows before releasing a visceral scream—a liberating act of release.

In a separate scenario, Dierdre, fortunate enough to possess a private office, found solace in the tranquil practice of yoga, dedicating a precious few minutes to untangling the knots of stress that accumulate throughout the day.

Then there's Jim, whose haven lies not in physical proximity but in the recesses of his mind. He mentally transports himself to the serene stream nestled near his summer abode, immersing his senses in the symphony of water cascading over the smooth, sun-kissed rocks—a mental oasis of peace.

For others, the path to tranquility unfolds through meditation or devout prayer, harnessing the power of mindfulness or spiritual connection to alleviate the burdens of workplace stress.

Each of these approaches, whether discovered through personal experimentation or embraced from existing practices, serves as a testament to the diverse arsenal available for stress reduction in the workplace. The key lies in uncovering a method that resonates with you, one that speaks to your unique needs and offers a personalized avenue to navigate the pressures of professional life.

'Holding on the anger is like grasping a hot coal
with the intent of throwing it at someone
else— you are the one who gets burned.'

—Buddha

USING YOUR POSITIVE ATTITUDE TO HELP OTHERS

Your pivotal role in rejuvenating a burnt-out member of your team cannot be overstated. Your own positive attitude serves as a beacon of hope, illuminating the path to their recovery through a series of transformative actions:

Firstly, displaying unwavering support is paramount. Engage in sincere conversations, fostering an environment where concerns are not only welcomed but actively addressed. Facilitate necessary adjustments, showcasing genuine interest in their well-being.

Consider the potential for a metamorphosis in job functions. Altering tasks or transitioning to a different team can invigorate their professional landscape, injecting freshness and offering novel avenues for rejuvenation.

Offering opportunities for skill acquisition is a dual-edged solution. Not only does it redirect focus towards learning, but it also augments their value within the company, fostering a sense of growth and accomplishment.

Should these interventions falter to yield progress, the prudent step is to advocate for professional counseling. This proactive approach can provide specialized guidance and support, acknowledging the complexity of the situation and offering targeted assistance.

Understanding your behavioural inclinations is merely the first step. Recognizing these tendencies acts as a clarion call, prompting proactive measures to cultivate a shift in attitude. By delving into the insights provided in this comprehensive guide and applying its principles, you pave the way to fortify yourself against stress and burnout. Embracing this journey involves a concerted effort to transmute negative thoughts into positive actions, a transformative process that, while demanding, yields invaluable rewards, promising a life enriched with newfound positivity and resilience.

'To be calm when others are not shifts the advantage to you in two ways:

—It stabilizes your position.

—It encourages allies impressed by your self-control.'

7

EFFECTIVE LEADERS ARE POSITIVE

'Looking back with regrets is a dangerous and self-defeating habit because it prevents a positive attitude. Move on!'

The teachings garnered from both triumphs and setbacks are intricately intertwined with one's attitude. Irrespective of your station—be it a CEO at the helm, a dedicated mail clerk or occupying a role somewhere in between—emulating the traits exhibited by triumphant leaders proves invaluable.

Venturing into the characteristics that epitomize successful leaders, it becomes apparent how a positive attitude serves as a linchpin to their accomplishments. These trailblazers exhibit a spectrum of qualities:

- They exhibit an impressive threshold for frustration, navigating challenges with resilience.
- Encouragement of active participation from others is a hallmark of their leadership.
- Continuous self-questioning propels their growth and evolution.
- Their competitiveness is marked by integrity and grace.
- Despite impulses, they refrain from retaliatory actions, displaying commendable self-control.

- Triumphs are celebrated with humility, devoid of boastfulness.
- Similarly, in moments of defeat, they exhibit resilience, eschewing despondency.
- The ethical, moral and legal compass guides their decisions and actions.
- Conscious of group dynamics, they nurture and value group loyalties.
- Realistic goal-setting underpins their strategies.

Whether steering a sizable team or embarking on the nascent stages of a career, gleaning insights from these successful leaders unveils the blueprint for ascending to pinnacles of achievement. A crucial aspect lies in realistic self-assessment, prompting the question, 'Do I passively await guidance or seize control of my personal development?'

Notably, those who ascend to greatness possess no divine mandate. Physically, emotionally, and intellectually, they bear resemblance to most of us. Their personalities, intelligence levels and methods of pursuing objectives are diverse.

Furthermore, a positive attitude serves as a catalyst, not only igniting personal drive but also kindling the same fervour in those around you. Channeling this enthusiasm to thrive and achieve is facilitated when you:

- Implement and actualize ideas, whether self-conceived or from others, by channeling them into pragmatic actions.
- Embrace accountability for actions and decisions.
- Exercise sound judgment with minimal internal turmoil.
- Prioritize facts over subjective opinions, meticulously gathering and interpreting data when problem-solving or seizing opportunities.
- Master the art of communication, fostering an atmosphere

where others feel heard and understood.
- Acknowledge the significance of others' roles and contributions.

Moreover, successful leaders exhibit adeptness in interpersonal relations. Often, technical incompetence isn't the primary stumbling block; rather, it's the inability to effectively collaborate with peers. Those adept at relating well have mastered the art of earning genuine respect by:

- Treating others with the same respect they desire.
- Acting as adept mentors and trainers.
- Offering constructive criticism.
- Exercising restraint over personal desires in favour of collective goals and harmony.

The qualities previously outlined serve merely as an introductory glimpse into the diverse array of attributes that successful leaders meticulously refine. Irrespective of your current standing within the organizational framework, the journey to master these traits is not only feasible but imperative for personal and professional growth.

Venturing beyond the aforementioned traits, other equally pivotal characteristics embody the very essence of triumphant leadership. Emulating these practices necessitates a deliberate focus on key arenas:

Carefully articulating and elucidating novel concepts or initiatives entails more than just unveiling ideas. It involves foreseeing potential hurdles, objections and apprehensions while empathizing with others' perspectives on change. Identifying and dismantling cooperation barriers becomes essential to successful implementation.

An essential aspect of this process involves acknowledging

the limitations of absolute answers. Redirecting inquiries toward constructive ends—solving, refining and enhancing—shifting away from the fruitless pursuit of assigning blame or fault.

Moreover, nurturing curiosity emerges as a cornerstone of effective leadership. Thriving leaders remain acutely attuned to evolving trends and advancements within their industry. Their preference for insightful reading over passive consumption through television enables a concentrated channeling of energy toward high-impact priorities—a habit ripe for adoption.

Courageously embracing calculated risks signifies delving into unexplored realms, exhibiting trust in individuals, navigating unorthodox situations and seeking innovative solutions, even at the potential expense of job security—an audacious step toward progress.

Further, leveraging humour to foster proactive engagement—a spirited call to action of 'let's do it'—stands as a potent instrument for effecting change and galvanizing collective effort. During transitional phases, these attributes serve as invaluable assets.

Crucially, prioritizing excellence over mediocrity emerges as a pivotal practice. It not only cultivates elevated job satisfaction but also kindles motivation and uplifts staff morale. Empowering employees to chart their career trajectories yields substantial dividends, even for those without managerial titles. Simple acts, such as expressing appreciation through emails highlighting exceptional contributions, can significantly elevate the workplace atmosphere.

Embracing the wisdom encapsulated by the adage, 'A positive attitude enables us to make up our minds against stalemates and in favour of progress,' embracing and embodying these qualities creates a robust framework to navigate challenges, catalyse progress, and propel both personal and collective growth toward unprecedented heights. This holistic approach underpins a transformative journey toward effective leadership and perpetual advancement.

BELIEVE IN YOURSELF

The bedrock of upholding a positive attitude rests upon an indomitable self-belief. Amidst these turbulent and unpredictable times, the notion of absolute certainty seems elusive, akin to chasing a fleeting mirage. Those who staunchly assert certainty often harbour a tint of pessimism, envisioning a perpetually darkening future. Strangely, this negativity can materialize as a self-fulfiling prophecy; pessimism spreads swiftly, colouring perceptions and ultimately shaping outcomes. It's a curious irony that what one believes to be impossible often materializes, the belief itself acting as the harbinger of its own fulfilment.

Reflect upon the timeless parable, 'The Man Who Sold Hot Dogs', a narrative likely birthed in the 1930s, yet resonates across ages:

Envision a humble vendor stationed by the roadside, vending hot dogs. Deafened by his hearing impairment and blind to worldly news due to vision troubles, he diligently sold his quality hot dogs. His persistent call, 'Buy a hot dog, Mister!' struck a chord, attracting customers. Witnessing success, he expanded operations, procured more supplies and even enlisted the aid of his college-educated son. However, a turning point arrived when his son, armed with worldly knowledge, painted a grim picture of global and domestic affairs. Yielding to his son's perspective, the father curtailed his operations, removed his signs, and halted roadside sales. As expected, hot dog sales plummeted overnight. Succumbing to prevailing pessimism, the father concurred with his son's appraisal, lamenting, 'You're right, son. We indeed find ourselves amidst a Great Depression.'

In an ambiance thick with despair, uncertainty often paralyses individuals, stifling the pursuit of the unknown sans assurances against potential pitfalls. This is where the axiom of destiny finds resonance: fleeting moments of glory pale against the enduring grasp of obscurity.

While uncertainty serves as a barricade for some, others assimilate it as an integral facet of life's journey. Certainty, a coveted treasure chest, finds no solid footing in reality, akin to the capriciousness of a racetrack. Life's absolutes dissolve into probabilities. Confident souls anticipate these probabilities to gradually align in their favour, akin to the ever-shifting odds on a gambling track.

This reservoir of confidence doesn't rely on external validations or guarantees of safety. Instead, it springs from an unwavering self-reliance rooted in personal convictions. It's about charting one's course, navigating the intricate labyrinth of uncertainty with unwavering self-assurance. Within this realm of assurance, dependency fades, supplanted by an unwavering trust in one's prowess and beliefs.

'A happy person is not a person in a certain set of circumstances, but rather a person with a certain set of attitudes.'

—Hugh Downs

THE IMPORTANCE OF HOW WE APPEAR TO OTHERS

'We awaken in others the same attitude of mind we hold toward them.'

—Elbert Hubbard

Self-assurance serves as the bedrock for fostering and projecting a positive attitude, yet the discrepancy between our internal feelings and external perceptions can often be stark. The disparity in how others perceive us vis-à-vis our self-perception underscores the critical need to harmonize these contrasting viewpoints. It's an intriguing paradox—why do certain individuals carry themselves with an air of solemnity? What drives them to derive overt satisfaction from parading their prestige and authority? Often, the root lies in insecurity. A lack of genuine confidence in their own worth compels them to constantly flaunt superiority and seek validation from others, masking their insecurities behind a façade of dominance.

Vanity presents another facet; the innate desire to feel important can sometimes spiral into uncontrolled egotism, leading to rather comical displays. Consider this note to serve as a whimsical reminder, 'Only two groups of people fall for flattery: men and women.' It's a gentle nudge to ground oneself periodically, ensuring a balanced perspective without soaring too high in the clouds of self-importance.

Shallowness can also drive individuals to inflate their significance, blinding them to the broader picture. This narrow focus often skews their understanding, distorting the reality of their role and impact.

It's not uncommon for individuals fostering a positive attitude to surge ahead and assume leadership roles. Why is this so? Their affirmative outlook equips them to navigate challenges more adeptly, enabling greater accomplishments at work and fostering contentment in their personal lives. Such individuals tend to command respect and attract followers due to their positive demeanour. When in positions of authority, they wield it not as a mark of superiority but as a means to achieve desired outcomes, all while maintaining a belief in equality, acknowledging the worth of those they lead.

Few things can be more exasperating than witnessing either a young or older person excessively consumed by their self-image. Hence, a gentle word of caution—should you find yourself veering toward either category, tread carefully! Awareness of this tendency serves as a safeguard against slipping into the pitfalls of taking oneself too seriously, irrespective of age or stage in life.

THE CHALLENGE OF LEADING

In a past role, I had the opportunity to collaborate with a Senior Vice President overseeing a robust $350 million retail store chain with ambitious aspirations to triple its sales within five years. Curious about the personal growth needed for such rapid expansion, I asked the Senior VP, 'What personal development do you foresee in achieving this remarkable growth?' His response was rather unexpected, 'I don't dwell on that. Frankly, I never envisioned reaching this level. I possess a substantial amount of self-assurance, so the future doesn't unsettle me.' His stance revealed a reluctance towards introspection and self-assessment, a crucial aspect in fostering growth. Furthermore, his lack of consideration for grooming potential successors signaled a disconnection from the evolving landscape. Despite his quarter-century of experience at that elevated position, he failed to grasp the fundamental truth that sustainable change must originate from within. It was intriguingly telling that his fellow executives didn't view him as promotable, highlighting the gap between his perception and the collective sentiment.

As the saying goes, 'Ideas are not rare. Making them useful is.' This adage encapsulates the essence of effective leadership. Whether steering a small-scale project or helming a corporate division, the fundamental objective remains consistent: attaining specific objectives through the collaborative efforts of others. Irrespective of the methodologies employed, the principal duty revolves around providing astute leadership to actualize envisioned outcomes. Despite its seeming simplicity, achieving this objective demands a series of exacting requirements and commitments.

Navigating the path of leadership, especially in steering a collective toward defined goals, is an intricate endeavour. The role extends far beyond superficial oversight; it encompasses fostering an environment that propels collective efforts toward a shared vision. It demands a delicate balance of strategic planning, effective communication, adept decision-making and, importantly, the ability to inspire and motivate individuals within the team.

Achieving objectives through others requires a multifaceted skill set, incorporating not just technical proficiency but also emotional intelligence and the capacity to inspire trust and confidence. It's a continuous journey of learning, adapting, and evolving—one where the focus remains resolutely on aligning actions with intended outcomes while nurturing a collaborative and cohesive team dynamic.

KEY FACTORS INVOLVED IN LEADERSHIP

Establishing an environment conducive to unlocking individuals' and teams' full potential is a pivotal responsibility for leaders. To achieve this, leaders must skillfully navigate several fundamental aspects:

Foremost, meticulous planning serves as the groundwork. However, the ability to remain adaptable and adept at improvisation in the face of the unexpected is equally essential.

Flexibility is the catalyst that enables leaders to steer their teams through uncharted territories, ensuring progress even amidst unforeseen challenges.

Effective leadership encompasses a dual role: innovator and executor. It involves not only the introduction of novel concepts and procedures but also the adept handling of day-to-day operations essential for maintaining the group's momentum. Striking this balance is a testament to a leader's prowess in maintaining both the forward momentum and the stability necessary for sustainable growth.

Crafting impactful questions stands as another cornerstone. Leaders who pose thought-provoking queries spark critical thinking, catalyse action and inspire continuous improvement within their teams. Skillfully crafted questions serve as the catalyst for innovation and progress.

Monitoring progress isn't merely about keeping a watchful eye; it's about orchestrating timely adaptations and recalibrations. Effective leaders constantly evaluate individual and group progress, swiftly implementing necessary changes and charting new courses of action to ensure alignment with overarching goals. This proactive approach ensures that both people and plans stay on track in an ever-evolving landscape.

Moreover, the art of persuasion reigns supreme over dominance. Effective communication skills lie at the heart of this aspect. Listening actively and responding articulately with clarity, simplicity and empathy is pivotal. Rather than imposing personal ideas, effective leaders skillfully persuade and inspire through their actions, leading by example and empowering others to follow suit.

In essence, effective leadership isn't a singular skill but a harmonious blend of adaptability, innovation, inquiry, proactive monitoring, and persuasive communication. It's about orchestrating a symphony of actions that inspire, motivate and guide individuals and teams toward shared objectives while fostering growth and development at every turn.

WHAT EFFECTIVENESS REQUIRES

'Winners mix optimism with opportunity.'

In the modern business arena, successful competitors are deeply committed to self-improvement and ongoing learning. They invest significant time in comprehending their organization's intricacies—its structures, policies and objectives—culminating in a comprehensive grasp of their responsibilities and lines of authority. Moreover, they possess a keen eye for identifying group dynamics and relationships, adeptly pinpointing opportunities for personal growth and supervisory development within their purview.

The essence of effective leadership extends far beyond acquiring knowledge; it demands a nuanced understanding of evolving trends and emerging patterns. Remaining stagnant in the face of rapid changes equates to falling behind the curve. Leaders who thrive amidst fierce competition exhibit distinctive traits:

They excel in interpersonal dynamics, adeptly managing teams to foster purposeful and harmonious organizational functioning. Their approach to problem-solving combines orderliness with a compassionate human touch, demonstrating thoughtfulness, tact and meticulousness. Amid their pursuit of heightened performance, they consistently garner the respect and admiration of those within their sphere.

Self-motivation is a defining trait—effective leaders manage themselves astutely, perpetually enhancing their skill sets and actively seeking novel ideas and methodologies.

Furthermore, a deep understanding of the dichotomy between efficiency and effectiveness sets them apart. While efficiency focuses on doing things right, effectiveness encompasses doing the right things right—balancing the pursuit of optimal outcomes with a discerning focus on achieving results that truly matter.

Identifying key result areas and gauging progress measures becomes crucial. Swift decision-making isn't the crux; instead, the best competitors meticulously strategize actions after careful consideration of what needs to be done. This deliberate approach ensures thoughtful action aligned with overarching goals.

Interestingly, a significant number of individuals lack a lucid understanding of their job requirements. A valuable exercise to assess performance priorities involves crafting concise answers to the question, 'What am I paid to accomplish?' Restricting each item to no more than four words, sans directional indicators or quantifiable measures, allows for a distilled yet comprehensive grasp of key objectives.

Evaluating these objectives against specific criteria—ensuring they represent output, align with responsibilities and authority, avoid overlap or underlaps with others' tasks, and integrate seamlessly both vertically and horizontally—serves as a litmus test for aligning personal objectives with organizational goals and the wider team structure. This exercise is pivotal in defining and refining performance priorities, facilitating strategic planning, and ensuring cohesive alignment with organizational objectives.

ARE YOU AN EFFECTIVE LEADER?

'The greatest risk is to risk nothing.'

Peter Drucker's pioneering work unveiled a distinctive set of attributes characterizing effective leaders. These qualities, as articulated by Drucker, remain pertinent in delineating what defines true leadership:

Firstly, leaders initiate projects by probing the fundamental question, 'What has to be done?' instead of centring on personal needs or desires. This proactive approach underscores a leader's focus on the collective objectives and the broader organizational goals rather than individual interests.

Continual introspection about the organization's overarching purposes and objectives is another hallmark of effective leadership. This ongoing questioning seeks clarity on acceptable performance benchmarks and contributions that tangibly add value to the organization's bottom line. Such a keen awareness ensures alignment with strategic goals and facilitates sustainable growth.

Moreover, true leaders eschew the inclination to mold replicas of themselves within their teams. They refrain from subjective judgments based on personal likes or dislikes but are unequivocal about tolerating poor performance. Their focus remains squarely on fostering a culture of excellence where performance is paramount.

A striking attribute of effective leaders lies in their lack of intimidation by others possessing strengths they themselves might lack. Instead of feeling threatened, they leverage the diversity of strengths within their team, recognizing that collective strengths forge a more resilient and versatile unit.

Interestingly, Drucker's astute observations on leadership characteristics seamlessly align with a contemporary understanding of competitiveness. By substituting the term 'competitors' for 'leaders' in Drucker's outlined qualities, a parallel emerges. Competitors, much like effective leaders:

Initiate projects with a focus on the essential tasks at hand, prioritizing collective goals over individual desires or needs.

Continuously evaluate their organization's objectives and performances, ensuring alignment with strategic imperatives that contribute tangibly to their competitive edge.

Avoid the trap of homogeneity by valuing performance over personal preferences, fostering a culture that upholds excellence.

Embrace diversity in strengths within their competitive landscape, leveraging varied competencies to bolster their own positions.

Drucker's astute observations transcend the realm of leadership, offering profound insights into the fabric of competitiveness. They underscore the importance of collective goals, performance-driven cultures and the strategic value of diversity in achieving and sustaining a competitive edge in any domain.

CARING CANNOT BE FAKED

Authentic care defies replication; it cannot be feigned or manufactured. Genuine concern for others forms a crucial cornerstone in cultivating a positive atmosphere around oneself. Yet, contemporary viewpoints on caring vary widely. Sceptics argue that modern society has witnessed a decline in genuine care, while others contend that there's an excess of self-absorption.

The subject of caring, however, remains enigmatic. Even social scientists admit to numerous unanswered questions. When and how do we acquire the capacity to care? Who assumes the role of caregivers? Does this sentiment hold relevance in business realms? Can one be taught to care?

According to Jack Beasley, Professor of Family and Child Studies at Georgia Southern College and a corporate consultant specializing in family issues, the ability to care is intertwined with one's inclination to perceive another's viewpoint or needs and respond accordingly. Beasley perceives caring as a skill, an attribute cultivated over a lifetime. Even if caring wasn't fostered during childhood, it's a trait that can be imbibed and honed in adulthood. Remarkably, many techniques integral to nurturing children's care capacities also amplify productivity and enrich relationships in professional settings.

For individuals aspiring to enhance their caring abilities, Professor Beasley advocates these starting techniques:

1. Observe individuals in scenarios where their team faces adversity or loss.
2. Showcase genuine care. Employees who perceive their supervisors and colleagues as caring tend to be more productive.
3. Exercise restraint. A crucial facet of caring is understanding when to step back. Provide appropriate care tailored to individual needs without overwhelming them. Avoid doing things for others that they can manage themselves, as excessive intervention may diminish both your value and their confidence.
4. Care enough to allow individuals to learn from logical consequences. While you can forewarn, firsthand experience often solidifies belief.
5. Maintain a balance between caring for others and managing your own needs. Care stems from self-esteem. Individuals at peace with themselves are less driven to prove themselves, unlike those grappling with self-identity. Encourage others to augment their abilities, allowing them to claim credit for their growth.
6. Lastly, practice self-care. Prioritizing self-care isn't selfish; it's essential. Without tending to your own well-being, demonstrating care for others becomes a challenge.

Embracing these techniques not only fosters an environment of genuine concern but also reinforces productivity, nurtures relationships, and bolsters personal growth—a testament to the profound impact of authentic care in both personal and professional spheres.

The repercussions of feigning care create a boomerang effect—one that often rebounds with adverse outcomes. Mark Twain's timeless wisdom encapsulates this notion succinctly, 'If you tell the truth, you don't have to remember anything.'

When insincerity permeates your care for others, it doesn't go unnoticed. People possess a remarkable ability to discern genuine concern from pretense. A lack of authentic care breeds demotivation and unhappiness among individuals. Conversely, when authentic care permeates your interactions, those around you take notice and reciprocate. Naturally, you find yourself inclined to:

- Challenge individuals with meaningful and purposeful work assignments.
- Acknowledge and appreciate their efforts by praising jobs well done.
- Uphold decisions that impact their well-being, standing firmly behind choices that affect their welfare.
- Pay meticulous attention to their genuine needs rather than assuming or imposing what you think they need.

For those in managerial positions or those aspiring to such roles, a critical introspection about the motives for pursuing management becomes imperative. Self-reflection about one's genuine interest in the welfare of their team members is essential. If the honest assessment yields a 'No' or an uncertain 'I'm not sure', attempting to feign care will yield little benefit. Simply put, genuine care cannot be counterfeited. Doubt about this fact can be settled by asking oneself, 'Among the pretenses I've encountered, who would I willingly follow?'

Honest evaluation and acknowledgment of one's motivations for leadership roles lay the foundation for genuine care and effective leadership. Attempting to masquerade or fake care only backfires, perpetuating a cycle of insincerity that ultimately undermines both personal and team growth.

8

MAXIMIZING YOUR PERFORMANCE

'For success, attitude is equally as important as ability.'

—Harry F. Banks

Attitude determines behaviour. The first question addressing this issue is, are you accountable?

ACCEPT RESPONSIBILITY FOR YOUR ACTIONS

Peter Drucker's insights on effective executive traits resonate profoundly in today's dynamic organizational landscapes. He underscores the significance of character development, foresight, self-reliance and courage among leaders. Drucker astutely highlights that organizations comprise ordinary individuals collectively tasked with achieving extraordinary feats. Yet, this ambition remains unattainable if individuals evade accountability.

Teaching accountability becomes imperative. While assuming responsibility may pose challenges, shying away from it for fear of making mistakes signifies failure. Long-term success hinges on the readiness to assume leadership when necessary, even at the risk of failure.

Infallible judgment eludes every individual. The fallibility of human judgment is exemplified in a narrative featuring a woman who ascended to a significant marketing position. In her initial assignment, she inadvertently made a severe error, resulting in a project failure and a staggering cost to the company—exceeding $100,000. When summoned by her boss, she apologized and presumed her termination was imminent. To her surprise, the boss's response was unexpected, 'Fire you? No way. I just invested $100,000 in your training.'

This anecdote poignantly illustrates the fallibility inherent in human decision-making. It elucidates the essential nature of acknowledging and learning from errors, rather than punishing individuals for their missteps. Such incidents often become pivotal learning moments, fostering growth and development.

Encouraging a culture where accountability is nurtured rather than penalized aids in cultivating a resilient workforce. It enables individuals to take calculated risks, fostering innovation and learning from setbacks. Ultimately, embracing accountability not only fosters a supportive environment but also propels organizational growth by transforming setbacks into valuable learning opportunities.

THINK BEFORE YOU DECIDE

The refinement of judgment is an ongoing process rooted in the disciplined consideration of fundamental aspects before making decisions. Instilling these practices can elevate your decision-making prowess:

- Deliberate and contemplate before acting hastily. When faced with a challenge, refrain from impulsive action. Take the time to methodically reason through the situation, striving to anticipate potential outcomes.

- For every potential solution, meticulously outline the pros and cons, costs, risks, as well as potential problems and objections that may arise.
- Embrace objectivity by scrutinizing the facts. Disregarding facts due to preconceived notions is a recipe for potential disaster.
- Keep biases, prejudices and personal preferences at bay. Empathize with others' perspectives. Consider how your decisions might impact your colleagues or associates. While an action may seem rational to you, how might it be perceived by others? Evaluating various perspectives is critical, as even the most well-conceived plans can falter if those involved are unwilling to cooperate. It's imperative to thoroughly explore all available avenues before determining the most prudent course of action.
- Acknowledge and accept criticism as an inherent part of the decision-making process.

By adhering to these guiding principles, one can refine their judgment, making more informed and considerate decisions. Incorporating these practices not only fortifies decision-making abilities but also fosters an environment of inclusive and thoughtful problem-solving.

EXPECT PROBLEMS

One prevalent shortcoming among managers is their tendency to evade confronting problems, preferring avoidance over assuming responsibility for decisive actions. This inclination to sidestep decisions stems from a fear of potential criticism and the belief that abstaining from making decisions shields them from any allegations of poor judgment.

A prominent president of a leading corporation, renowned for nurturing the development of associates, has a distinct approach to handling errors in judgment. His standard response to most instances of misjudgment is a resolute, 'All right, that's behind us; now what's our next move?' This approach underscores his emphasis on propelling forward momentum, urging individuals to actively make decisions and managers to effectively manage. His underlying ethos prioritizes action and values a track record of consistent achievement over apprehension caused by the fear of making mistakes. Notably, the outcomes illustrate that his approach frequently yields the desired results.

In essence, this approach underscores a fundamental truth: life resembles a batting average more than a perfect scorecard. It acknowledges that imperfection is an integral part of the journey toward progress and success. Embracing this philosophy fosters an environment where decisiveness is valued, mistakes are seen as learning opportunities and forward momentum is prioritized over the fear of making errors. This approach often catalyses a culture of continuous improvement, allowing organizations to evolve and thrive amid challenges.

'What happens to us is less important than what we make happen.'

PERCEPTION CAN BE REALITY

Communication in the workplace holds immense significance, regardless of one's position on the managerial hierarchy. Beyond the content of what you convey, the manner in which you express yourself carries equal weight. Your attitude toward employees and co-workers reverberates loudly in the workplace. People often wonder about the intent behind directives, 'Is this task just busywork? Am I a dumping ground for my boss's unfinished business? Will my effort contribute meaningfully?'

The approach you adopt while assigning tasks can significantly impact how your directives are perceived. Simply dictating without providing context or rationale can lead to misunderstandings and diminished morale. Therefore, it's pivotal to articulate the 'why' alongside the 'what' when delegating responsibilities. This act of offering explanations stands as an invaluable practice, despite the apparent expediency of straightforward commands.

When you elucidate the rationale behind a request, you transcend the realm of bossiness. By providing a compelling reason for the task, you transform directives into logical and reasonable requests, fostering a more collaborative and understanding environment.

Moreover, communicating the 'why' behind tasks serves as a proactive measure against errors. Individuals equipped with a clear understanding of the purpose are less prone to mistakes. Additionally, in dynamic scenarios where circumstances change, this understanding empowers them to adapt and communicate back if the original action is no longer warranted.

Failure to provide adequate context can lead to misinterpretation or blind adherence to instructions, fostering a culture where individuals merely execute orders without engaging their critical thinking skills. This absence of elucidation can inadvertently create a scapegoat scenario, where errors are attributed to miscommunication rather than constructive dialogue.

By explaining the rationale, you impart a sense of trust and respect to your team members. It showcases the importance you place on clarity, background insight and encourages them to engage their analytical faculties. This approach isn't just about relaying instructions; it's about fostering an environment where individuals feel valued and empowered to offer suggestions, thereby contributing meaningfully to the task at hand.

Granted, there are instances where reasons may seem self-evident or urgent, requiring immediate action. However, as a guiding principle, providing explanations stands as a cornerstone of effective leadership and collaboration, fostering a culture of mutual understanding and productivity in the workplace.

KNOW YOUR COLLEAGUES

An in-depth examination of individuals who have ascended the ladder of success within the business realm frequently reveals the presence of four key factors:

- **Deliberative Action:** successful individuals display an inclination to contemplate and analyse before embarking on actions or decisions.
- **Intrinsic Motivation:** they possess an innate drive and passion that propels them forward, fueling their endeavours with determination and persistence.
- **Readiness for Accountability:** successful individuals willingly shoulder responsibility, demonstrating ownership of their actions and decisions.
- **Leadership Acumen:** they exhibit the ability to inspire and lead people, recognizing and leveraging talents within teams to achieve shared goals.

In the dynamic landscape of organizations, individuals evolve—some grow, while others stagnate, succumbing to complacency and disinterest. A challenge for effective leadership is to remain attuned to these shifts, acknowledging and nurturing the burgeoning talents of employees, even amidst changing circumstances.

Long-serving employees, who have dutifully executed their roles for an extended period, might inadvertently fade into the background due to their reliability. Yet, their potential for growth and capability might surpass their current roles. Many have outgrown their positions and await an opportunity for expansion and advancement.

One key aspect often overlooked is the need for organizations to perceive their employees with fresh eyes periodically. Employees who seem settled in their roles might harbour untapped potential or readiness for greater challenges. Organizations should avoid the pitfall of confining individuals within roles they have surpassed. It's detrimental both to their personal growth and the company's progress.

While workload prioritization is crucial, it's equally vital to identify avenues for providing additional challenges to capable individuals. For those excelling in their current roles, it's pertinent to explore opportunities for diversification. Can their skill set be further tested with new responsibilities? Can their expertise be expanded by tackling fresh challenges in their area of specialization?

Employers should aim not to underestimate their employees' potential. It's imperative to envision individuals thriving in more demanding scenarios. What matters isn't just their past capabilities but their present and future potential.

A telling case involves H. Ross Perot's engagement with GM. Perot, a successful maverick, was brought in by GM at a time when the company's market share was dwindling. Despite his insights and successful track record, GM's entrenched management hesitated to embrace new perspectives and innovation, leading to missed opportunities. The clash between innovation and resistance to change ultimately resulted in a status quo bias.

This story underscores the importance of recognizing fresh

perspectives and the potential for growth within an organization. Embracing change and fostering a culture receptive to new ideas often pave the way for sustained progress and success.

> *'Encourage your associates to express their ideas, especially when they differ from yours. Their disagreements not only provide you with new ideas, but give you insight into the way they approach problems that will help you work more effectively with them.'*
>
> —Franklin C. Ashby

POSITIVE ATTITUDE ENCOURAGES IMPROVED PERFORMANCE

Let's delve deeper into the impact of attitude on workplace productivity and explore the multifaceted aspects of effective managerial practices:

Beyond its effects on morale, self-esteem and behaviour, the attitude prevailing in a workplace directly intersects with the company's bottom line. As a manager, your role extends beyond supervision; it involves fostering an environment that optimizes employee productivity. Here are foundational suggestions to achieve this:

1. **Champion Innovative Ideas:** act as a conduit, relaying progressive suggestions and innovative ideas from coworkers and team members to upper management. Encourage a culture where fresh thinking is valued and acknowledged.
2. **Foster Creativity:** cultivate an environment where creative thinking is nurtured, ensuring that individuals feel safe to share their novel ideas without fear of ridicule or criticism. Creativity often flourishes in an atmosphere of acceptance and open-mindedness.

3. **Credit Where It's Due:** acknowledge the originators of ideas. When you credit individuals for their contributions instead of claiming their ideas as your own, it not only recognizes their efforts but also incentivizes them to generate more innovative solutions.
4. **Purposeful Work Assignments:** provide tasks that employees find meaningful and impactful. A sense of achievement stemming from completing significant assignments that contribute tangibly to the company's growth can be a powerful motivator.
5. **Foster a Sense of Belonging:** help employees understand the unique and special aspects of being part of your organization. Creating a sense of belonging can forge stronger bonds and commitment among team members.
6. **Highlight Significance:** encourage contemplation about the importance of the work undertaken by your team. Sometimes, employees undervalue their work due to a perceived lack of appreciation or acknowledgment from others.
7. **Beyond Monetary Rewards:** while financial compensation is essential, recognize that employees seek more than just monetary rewards. Participation, recognition, a sense of belonging and the opportunity for achievement carry significant weight. When these aspects are cultivated within a fair compensation framework, the singular pursuit of money takes a backseat.

By implementing these strategies, managers can create an environment where employees not only feel valued and recognized but also find purpose and fulfilment in their work. This holistic approach contributes to a more engaged and motivated workforce, ultimately impacting the organization's overall success.

'Ability is what you're capable of doing. Motivation determines what you do. Attitude determines how well you do it.'

—Lou Holtz

THE GENERATION GAP

Professor Quinn Mills, through extensive research conducted at Harvard University, has shed light on the significant differences in work attitudes among various generations. While ethnic backgrounds and job sectors do not seem to influence values significantly, age differences stand out prominently in shaping workplace perceptions.

1. **Authority Acceptance:** the older generation, shaped by the aftermath of World War II, tends to embrace authority figures. Contrastingly, the 'baby boomers'—representative of the younger generation raised during the Vietnam era—exhibit a general scepticism towards authority figures, expressing a lack of trust.
2. **Perception of Work:** work ethos differs notably between generations. The older cohort views work as a solemn duty, a means to support themselves and their families. On the contrary, the younger generation views work as an arena for enjoyment, social interaction and fun. It has become a pivotal social space alongside other recreational areas like health clubs.
3. **Promotion and Performance:** perspectives on career advancement vary distinctly. The older generation perceives experience as the crucial pathway to advancement, willing to invest time in apprenticeships with the expectation of rewards. In contrast, the younger generation believes in swift progress in alignment with their performance,

questioning the need for waiting periods.

4. **Communication Styles:** differences in communication styles are apparent. The older generation often values tact, whereas the younger generation prioritizes honesty and directness, viewing tact as a form of evasion rather than a diplomatic approach.
5. **Fairness and Individuality:** while the older generation associates fairness with treating everyone equally, the younger generation advocates for fairness by allowing individuality and embracing differences among individuals.
6. **Value Focus:** the older generation tends to focus on possessions and status as markers of success, while the younger generation values experiences and personal fulfilment over material possessions.

Understanding and acknowledging these generational disparities in work attitudes is crucial for fostering a harmonious and productive work environment. Employers and managers can leverage this knowledge to bridge gaps, promote collaboration and adapt work structures to accommodate diverse perspectives, thereby enhancing overall workplace satisfaction and performance.

Considering the evolving landscape of generational dynamics in the workplace is paramount, given the shift from the WWII generation to the baby boomer cohort, now occupying key managerial roles. With subsequent generations like Gen-X and Gen-Y—their children and grandchildren—entering the workforce, there's a noticeable departure in outlook and values. These newer generations often exhibit independent thinking and a certain resistance to traditional authority structures.

Managers in the current era need to immerse themselves in understanding the unique expectations and attitudes of these younger generations to effectively engage and manage them. This grasp becomes especially crucial as the proportion of younger individuals in the workforce diminishes, leading to potential labour shortages and heightening the significance of addressing generational gaps.

Interestingly, there are hidden advantages in the inexperience of younger recruits, contrary to common scepticism. Take the perspective of Patrick Kelly and Bill Riddell from Physician Sales and Services, Inc., who see the potential in leveraging inexperience. They believe that certain routine tasks can be infused with a remarkable level of enthusiasm when entrusted to inexperienced individuals, provided there's a clear plan for their growth and advancement within the organization.

This approach acknowledges that fresh minds, unburdened by entrenched practices or preconceptions, might approach routine tasks with a vigour and open-mindedness that can infuse new energy into the workplace. The key lies in providing a clear path for their development, aligning their roles with growth opportunities and fostering an environment that values their contribution, irrespective of their relative inexperience in the industry.

Harnessing the potential of inexperienced individuals by nurturing their enthusiasm and potential can be an effective strategy, particularly in reshaping mundane tasks into engaging opportunities for growth and development. This approach not only revitalizes routine roles but also cultivates a culture that encourages progress and evolution, benefiting both the organization and the individuals involved.

Hiring inexperienced individuals often presents an opportunity to infuse fresh perspectives and enthusiasm into the workforce. Take the approach of leaders like Riddell, who understand the potential of recruiting and training young talent. Riddell's strategy involves convincing these individuals that their current roles are temporary, with a reasonable expectation of transitioning to new responsibilities in as little as six months. This approach yields highly motivated team members willing to take on diverse tasks, from driving delivery vans to performing janitorial duties.

Furthermore, Riddell emphasizes the importance of instilling a distinct company culture among recruits, particularly those who bring prior experience from other organizations. Many individuals, having imbibed different workplace attitudes, need to 'unlearn' certain habits or approaches before they can fully embrace the ethos of their new workplace. It's about fostering a culture that aligns with the company's values and vision, which can sometimes necessitate a reorientation for seasoned professionals.

In fact, Riddell has observed that hiring inexperienced individuals facilitates the dissemination and assimilation of the company culture more efficiently. When experienced hires are brought on board, they're often surrounded by less experienced colleagues. This intentional mix accelerates the process of steering the work culture in the desired direction, aligning it more swiftly with the company's overarching goals and values.

Enterprise Rent-a-Car similarly embraces a similar philosophy in its recruitment strategy. The company annually hires thousands of management trainees from diverse global campuses. These recruits start from the bottom rung, performing tasks like car washing and customer pickups. However, those who excel in these seemingly mundane roles do so with enthusiasm because they recognize the potential for rapid career advancement within the organization.

This model, seen in Riddell's approach and Enterprise Rent-a-Car's recruitment philosophy, demonstrates how embracing inexperienced talent and nurturing them within the company culture can not only infuse energy but also pave the way for swift career progression. It underscores the significance of providing opportunities for growth and development, irrespective of the entry-level nature of the initial tasks, ultimately fostering a culture of upward mobility and ambition within the organization.

'He who would accomplish little must sacrifice little. He who would accomplish much must sacrifice much.'

—James Allen

9

SHARPENING YOUR INTERPERSONAL SKILLS

A positive attitude can be a game-changer in navigating through various options effectively. Yet, the workplace often grapples with issues stemming not from technical prowess but rather from the lack of essential people skills. The dynamics of how you interact with colleagues can indeed dictate the trajectory of success or failure within an organization. Surprisingly, many workplace dilemmas, though they may appear complex, can be rectified with simple yet impactful actions.

Consideration for others lies at the core of fostering a harmonious workplace. It's reflected in punctuality, respecting allocated meal and break times, minimizing personal calls or emails, leaving personal issues outside the workplace, showing respect for others' belongings, adhering to dress codes, maintaining confidentiality and steering clear of detrimental office gossip. These seemingly basic actions collectively contribute significantly to a conducive work environment.

Moreover, proactive communication about areas of concern, long before they snowball into insurmountable issues, is pivotal. Addressing issues at their inception avoids the trap of allowing minor problems to escalate into full-blown crises where rectification becomes challenging.

Another key aspect is seizing the initiative. While respecting the hierarchical structure is crucial, offering a helping hand or support to colleagues when appropriate can foster a collaborative atmosphere. This demonstrates a willingness to go beyond set boundaries to contribute positively to the team's success.

In essence, these seemingly simple actions—displaying consideration, proactive communication and taking initiative—form the bedrock of effective workplace interactions. They serve as the linchpin for a harmonious environment, mitigating potential conflicts and fostering a culture of mutual respect and cooperation. Embracing these principles not only enhances individual relationships but also contributes significantly to the collective success of the organization.

> *'Pretend that every single person you meet has a sign around his or her neck that says MAKE ME FEEL IMPORTANT. Not only will you succeed in sales, you will succeed in life.'*
>
> —Mary Kaye Ash

PREPARING FOR CHANGE

The relationship between progress and change is often inseparable. Your attitude towards change significantly influences how you handle it and how effectively you prepare for it.

Change, let's be honest, is rarely comfortable. It tends to stir up feelings of uncertainty and unease, leading us to question whether maintaining the status quo might be a better choice. Despite this initial hesitation, embracing new ideas becomes paramount in remaining competitive and staying ahead of the curve. Here are some strategies that can ease the transition:

Embracing Change

Change is often best introduced gradually, presenting new ideas not as radical departures but as potential options worthy of consideration. Highlighting their similarities with past successful practices or current approaches gives individuals the chance to ponder these ideas before revisiting them.

Nurturing Acceptance

Further, gently underscoring the additional benefits of these new concepts without applying excessive pressure helps foster open discussions. It's crucial to value diverse opinions and consider implementing changes in smaller increments over time, rather than executing a significant overhaul all at once.

Handling Resistance

In the face of significant resistance, temporarily stepping back from pushing the change might prove wise. Instead of abandoning the idea altogether, reframing or reintroducing it at a more opportune time or under different circumstances can enhance acceptance. Logical arguments might not always win hearts, so gaining genuine support for change is more effective in the long run.

Preparing for Change

Recognizing the intricacies and challenges change presents is crucial. Cultivating a positive outlook toward change not only assists in personal adaptation but also influences those around you, easing the transition into new operational methods.

Navigating change isn't just about embracing new ideas—it's about fostering an environment where change is seen as an opportunity rather than a threat. This positive perspective influences how change is perceived and embraced across the workplace.

OVERCOMING RESISTANCE TO CHANGE

Resistance to change within a work environment manifests in numerous ways, which become apparent through various observable behaviours. These include an uptick in absenteeism, an increase in the rate of employee turnover, a surge in requests for transfers, a rise in complaints, a decrease in cooperation among team members, hesitancy towards supporting newly introduced systems and a noticeable decline in overall productivity.

The visible forms of resistance often emanate from changes that could potentially lead to job insecurity, a devaluation of individual skills or a reduction in compensation. These concerns regarding personal consequences serve as significant catalysts for resistance towards embracing new initiatives or any alterations in the established organizational structure.

To garner continual backing for novel ideas or alterations, two essential approaches emerge as pivotal: firstly, fostering an environment that encourages active involvement and participation, and secondly, taking proactive steps to address and alleviate any brewing feelings of resentment. These strategic methods not only facilitate the introduction of change but also ensure its smooth assimilation within the workplace culture, leading to greater acceptance and successful integration.

ENCOURAGE PARTICIPATION

Acknowledging and addressing the lingering issues within your work environment is a crucial step toward progress. Identifying these persistent challenges allows for a clearer understanding of their underlying causes, enabling a more targeted approach to resolution. It's pivotal to initiate action and work toward solutions once these concerns are identified.

In the pursuit of problem-solving or even routine tasks, actively seeking suggestions plays a pivotal role in achieving ultimate success. Esteemed leaders recognize and embrace the fact that most individuals possess valuable insights and innovative ideas. However, the absence of suggestions from employees often stems from an environment where their input isn't actively sought or appreciated by their managers. Consequently, this lack of encouragement stifles the generation of new and more effective approaches to tasks or problems.

It's imperative to tap into the wealth of knowledge and experiences of those directly involved in day-to-day operations. With a little encouragement, individuals can offer invaluable suggestions for improvement. Successful leaders understand that the frontline staff, engaged in the daily execution of tasks, often harbour the best ideas on enhancing processes or operations.

The efficacy of leaders isn't solely measured by their own performance but also by the collective efforts of their team. Managers who foster an environment conducive to innovation and idea-sharing tend to unlock their team's full potential, driving progress and growth within the organization.

It's noticeable that astute managers often have proficient assistants, not by happenstance but due to deliberate efforts to develop them. Encouraging critical thinking and fostering a sense of responsibility among team members pave the way for individual and collective growth.

One of the most straightforward yet effective ways to stimulate a flow of suggestions is simply by soliciting them. Engaging the people involved in discussions about existing problems or challenges often yields a pool of innovative ideas and solutions. Appreciating and valuing these contributions fosters an environment of collaboration and empowerment.

Lastly, demonstrating gratitude for the suggestions received, coupled with thoughtful consideration before responding, not only acknowledges the efforts of contributors but also signifies a genuine commitment to evaluating and implementing viable ideas.

REJECTING SUGGESTIONS WITHOUT CAUSING RESENTMENT

Margo Marston convened her team to address an issue, and during this session, Diane, a recent addition to the team, suggested a potential solution. However, Margo's immediate response, albeit based on past unsuccessful attempts at a similar idea, was a flat-out dismissal, 'We tried that before and it didn't work.' While it was accurate that such an attempt had faced challenges previously, Diane perceived this as a rejection of her ideas and felt disheartened. She not only harboured resentment but also grew hesitant about presenting future ideas, convinced they'd meet the same fate of automatic rejection.

So, how could Margo have approached this situation differently, rejecting the idea without causing such a negative reaction in Diane?

One approach involves handling such situations privately. Rejecting suggestions in a group setting should be avoided at all costs. Instead, Margo could have thanked Diane for her input, expressing the intent to review it further. Later, in a one-on-one discussion, Margo could have delicately explained the prior unsuccessful attempt by saying,'We had serious problems with it.' This choice of phrasing leaves the door open for further discussion and potential improvement. Diane might have responded differently, perhaps acknowledging overlooked aspects or proposing modifications to address previous issues.

Another effective strategy involves asking pertinent questions. In the vein of the great teacher Socrates, who never declared a student's response as incorrect outright but prodded them with thought-provoking questions, Margo could have guided Diane's thinking process. Skillfully worded questions could have prompted Diane to reconsider her initial idea, encouraging her to reassess and refine it into a more viable solution.

When it comes to turning down suggestions, a gentle approach is key. It's crucial to convey unequivocal appreciation for the ideas presented while emphasizing the desire for further contributions. This attitude fosters an environment where individuals feel valued and motivated to keep sharing, knowing that their next idea might just be the breakthrough solution.

'Give thanks and celebrate a positive attitude.
It enables you to test your potential every day.'

10

HOW ATTITUDE AFFECTS RESULTS

'I am not saying a Positive Attitude can make you successful. I am saying a Positive Attitude will make you successful.'

—Norman Vincent Peale

Understanding the pivotal role of a boss in one's job satisfaction and career development is paramount. Whether fortunate enough to work under an exemplary leader, mentor and teacher or dealing with an opposite scenario, an individual's approach towards their supervisor significantly influences their job experience.

Adapting and tailoring one's actions to align with the boss's objectives, style and work practices can maximize the work dynamic. Linda's experience in the Purchasing Department vividly illustrates this point. Upon recognizing Carol's meticulous nature and her preference for a structured work environment, Linda made conscious adjustments. She observed Carol's punctuality and organization, traits that diverged from her prior boss's style. Determined to adapt, Linda altered her work habits, arriving earlier, organizing her workspace meticulously, and adjusting her attire to mirror a more conservative approach.

This proactive adaptation laid the foundation for a

successful rapport with Carol, fostering a harmonious and productive working relationship. Linda's willingness to adjust her work practices to sync with her supervisor's expectations not only facilitated a positive work environment but also paved the way for her career growth and swift advancement within the department.

DO'S AND DON'T'S IN DEALING WITH YOUR BOSS

Here are foundational guidelines that can aid in crafting effective coping mechanisms for handling interactions with your supervisor:

The Do's

- Consider observing and learning from those individuals who maintain a positive relationship with your boss. Their methods of coping and navigating workplace dynamics can serve as valuable lessons to emulate and follow.
- Acknowledge the possibility that your role might contribute to the strained relationship with your supervisor, if there's one. Recognize the shared responsibility in the equation, knowing that while you can't change your boss, you can modify your behaviour. Take accountability and initiate actions to foster positive changes.
- Offer to handle tasks that your supervisor might not favour, thereby contributing to easing their workload.
- Stay attuned to your boss's patterns of mood swings, noting the times of the day or week when they seem more open and approachable.
- Express your sentiments about your boss's treatment of

you. However, ensure the timing is appropriate, waiting until your boss has cooled down and discuss your feelings calmly and privately.

- Monitor your progress. If you're not achieving the desired results, reassess your approach in dealing with your supervisor. Adjust your strategy if necessary, bearing in mind that changes might take time to yield noticeable effects. Be patient and persistent, understanding that progress is a gradual process.

The Don't's

- Avoid engaging in disputes over your employer's authority, even if you harbour a different viewpoint regarding their judgment in a particular scenario. Upholding their authority, especially during disagreements, maintains a professional decorum within the workplace.
- Resist interpreting criticism as a personal affront. Distinguishing between your job responsibilities, which might be manageable and your boss's behaviour that doesn't meet your expectations can help maintain professional equilibrium.
- Refrain from constantly seeking your boss' approval for every action. Taking initiative and executing tasks as necessary demonstrates autonomy while keeping your boss informed afterward.
- Steer clear of participating in gossip or negative talk about your boss behind their back. Displaying loyalty and professionalism in all interactions fosters a respectful work environment.
- Avoid bypassing your boss's authority, except in urgent circumstances like emergencies. Disregarding the

established chain of command often leads to complexities rather than resolving issues.

- Prioritize your self-respect above all. If your coping strategies have proven ineffective and a transfer isn't feasible, preserving your self-esteem becomes crucial. If needed, explore opportunities for a new job under a different supervisor to ensure your professional dignity and fulfilment.

Remember, forming conclusive judgments about individuals should rely not just on their words or intentions, but on observed evidence and the actual outcomes of their actions and behaviour.

IDENTIFY ACCOUNTABLE PEOPLE

Evaluating the success of a business often reveals that financial insufficiency isn't the primary cause of failure. Rather, it frequently stems from realizing too late that the wrong individuals have been engaged in pivotal roles. Assessing the dynamics within your professional circle—comprising your boss, colleagues and employees—becomes crucial in understanding their impact on your success trajectory.

While financial resources are undoubtedly vital, the people factor remains a linchpin in achieving business objectives. The attitudes, skills and motivations of those around you can significantly influence the overall efficacy of your efforts. Therefore, it's imperative to carefully consider the roles played by each person within your professional network.

Your boss, for instance, holds a pivotal position in guiding your work environment and setting the tone for collaboration and productivity. Colleagues contribute to the collective synergy, potentially fostering innovation or, conversely, creating obstacles that hinder progress. Additionally, your employees significantly shape the execution of tasks and the attainment of goals.

Assessing whether these individuals align with your vision, provide constructive support and actively contribute to the collective success is crucial. Recognizing whether they empower or impede progress can help guide your decisions, ensuring a conducive environment for growth and success.

THE LEAST VALUABLE PEOPLE (LVP) PROFILE

This checklist, my 'Least Valuable People' profile, has proven instrumental in identifying behavioural patterns that might lead to failure or, conversely, forecast success among individuals. It's an effective tool for gauging personal attributes crucial for professional advancement or setback.

Its simplicity lies in the binary nature of responses: Guilty or Not Guilty. This straightforward approach makes self-assessment and assessment of others relatively easy. Starting by evaluating oneself allows for introspection before evaluating others.

Here's where it gets intriguing. The traits listed are indicative of attitudes and behaviours that either propel someone toward success or hinder their progress. For instance, avoiding problems, blaming others for failures or failing to meet deadlines might signify a lack of accountability and initiative. Conversely, proactively seeking clarification, taking risks and fostering talent are traits associated with successful individuals.

By analysing these traits, individuals can gauge where they stand in terms of attitude and approach to work. It helps differentiate between behaviours that contribute to success and those that lead to failure. Identifying these attributes aids in self-improvement and assists in making informed decisions about whom to align with in a professional setting.

Start by rating yourself first.

Guilty or Not Guilty

1. Constantly sidesteps problems and complaints, hoping someone else will handle them. ____________
2. Avoids disciplining people. ____________
3. Blames others when things go wrong. ____________
4. Allows false statements to go unchallenged. ____________
5. Doesn't worry about being late for work or meetings. ____________
6. Postpones completion of projects as long as possible. ____________
7. Avoids seeking clarification of misunderstandings in order to criticize later. ____________
8. Never volunteers for an assignment when not absolutely certain of success. ____________
9. Doesn't worry about deadlines. ____________
10. Maintains the same sources of information and bases decisions more on opinions than facts. ____________
11. Tries to be as noncommittal as possible. ____________
12. Punishes good people who disagree. ____________
13. Sees delegating as a way of getting rid of unpleasant chores rather than improving and expanding productivity. ____________
14. Keeps busy on current projects and is uncomfortable about future planning. ____________
15. Allows someone else to do recruiting and selection. ____________
16. Tends to criticize others in public, rather than in private. ____________
17. Is insulated from contact with customers. ____________

18. Frequently talks about how much others depend on them. ____________
19. Is not concerned about nurturing promotable people. ____________
20. Is uncomfortable when depending on others to provide answers. ____________
21. Concentrates efforts on favourite tasks rather than highest priorities. ____________
22. Rarely compliments others for their good work. ____________
23. Downplays the competence of other people. ____________
24. Takes as few risks as possible. ____________
25. Waits as long as possible before delivering bad news. ____________
26. Limits efforts to 'on-the-job' hours; rarely takes work home. ____________
27. Is not involved in self-improvement programs. ____________
28. Joins in conversations about the 'good old days' as often as possible. ____________
29. Talks a lot about how difficult it is to objectively measure what they do. ____________
30. Hides talented people to further their own career. ____________

When reviewing the results of your responses, the number of 'Guilty' verdicts could offer valuable insights into the behavioural tendencies that may shape your or someone else's professional trajectory. Here's a breakdown of the assessment based on the number of 'Guilty' verdicts:

0–4 Guilty verdicts: this suggests a commendable level of accountability and responsibility. Individuals falling within this range are invaluable assets. It's crucial to retain and nurture their contributions to your team or organization.

5–10 Guilty verdicts: individuals within this bracket display a mix of positive and concerning traits. With appropriate guidance and support, they have the potential to evolve and handle increased responsibilities. Mentorship and coaching can facilitate their growth and development.

11–20 Guilty verdicts: Individuals with numerous 'Guilty' verdicts require careful observation. Their actions may pose potential risks to your organization's efficiency and success. It's advisable to monitor their behaviour closely and address problematic areas promptly.

More than 20 Guilty verdicts: a high count of 'Guilty' verdicts indicates significant concerns in behaviour and attitude. Such individuals might pose severe challenges and risks to the organization. If you're their supervisor, maintaining documented records of their problematic behaviour and seeking guidance from Human Resources could be a wise approach. As a co-worker, it's advisable to minimize interactions. If this person is your supervisor, maintaining professionalism while exploring a transfer might be beneficial.

By interpreting these results, you gain valuable insights into the potential impact of individual behaviours and can make informed decisions about collaboration, mentorship or taking proactive steps to address concerning patterns.

GET THE HELP YOU NEED

'Keep away from people who try to belittle your ambitions. Small people always do that, but the really great make you feel that you too can become great.'

—Mark Twain

Acknowledging vulnerability in reliance on others' performance is a hallmark of successful individuals. They understand the profound impact those around them can have on their own success, be it their team, colleagues or mentors and superiors. Surrounding oneself with individuals who uplift and complement capabilities becomes a strategic move in fostering personal and collective growth.

Utilizing the insights from the LVP (Least Valuable People) profile isn't just about identifying problematic situations; it's also a means to recognize the potential of those who exhibit exceptional qualities:

1. **Going Beyond Expectations:** remarkable individuals don't settle once they've met the status quo. They continuously strive for progress beyond existing benchmarks.
2. **Solution-Oriented:** instead of presenting problems, they propose solutions. Their approach is collaborative, framing challenges as collective issues and offering recommendations to resolve them.
3. **Resilience in Mistakes:** rather than blaming others, they own up to their mistakes and exhibit resilience. They explore alternative approaches to overcome errors.
4. **Accountability Without Excuses:** when things go wrong, they take responsibility and focus on resolving the issue rather than making excuses.
5. **Self-Management:** they proactively manage their tasks, setting interim deadlines for long-term projects, eliminating last-minute panic.
6. **Striving for Improvement:** instead of chasing perfection, they prioritize growth and improvement. Perfectionism often leads to undue pressure and frustration, hindering actual accomplishments.

7. **Foresight and Planning:** forward-thinking individuals anticipate challenges and plan ahead, minimizing the occurrence of unpleasant surprises.
8. **Forward Momentum:** they refrain from dwelling excessively on past successes or dwelling on errors. Instead, they swiftly pivot from both triumphs and missteps, focusing on the current task or future objectives. This ability to move forward rapidly fosters an environment of continuous improvement and growth.
9. **Inquisitiveness**: they understand the importance of seeking clarity. When uncertainty arises, they actively seek clarification rather than assuming. This practice ensures that information is accurate and reduces the likelihood of misunderstandings or errors.
10. **Proactivity in Decision-Making**: successful individuals are proactive in decision-making. They negotiate agreements and promptly take action. They don't wait for explicit instructions to proceed; once negotiations are settled, they initiate actions aligned with the agreed-upon terms. This proactive approach accelerates progress and innovation within their roles.

In any organization, individuals who initiate, negotiate and share knowledge are invaluable assets. These qualities—initiation, negotiation, and teaching—are essential for driving progress, resolving conflicts and fostering growth. Recognizing, recruiting, retaining and collaborating more with individuals who exhibit strength in these areas significantly enhances the likelihood of achieving organizational success. Their ability to initiate actions, facilitate agreements and impart knowledge empowers the entire team, propelling the organization toward its goals and reinforcing a culture of productivity and collaboration.

Identifying these traits enables you not only to steer clear of potential problems but also to recognize and foster relationships with individuals whose characteristics align with success-oriented behaviours. Collaborating with such individuals can elevate overall team performance and contribute significantly to achieving collective objectives.

WHAT'S WRONG VS. WHO'S WRONG

It's vital to delve deeper into the nuances of responsibility and attitude, especially concerning the focus on problems and accountability within an organizational context.

The distinction between concentrating on what is wrong versus who is wrong embodies a significant element of a positive attitude and accountability. Focusing on 'who' implies a constant search for someone to hold accountable or blame when things go awry. This perspective creates an atmosphere rife with tension and defensiveness. When an environment is shadowed by a blame-seeking culture, it can foster a defensive stance among team members. Everyone becomes apprehensive, anticipating the next round of accusations or finger-pointing.

Contrastingly, concentrating on 'what' went wrong directs attention toward understanding the problem itself. It's about analysing the issue, identifying the root cause and finding constructive solutions. This approach fosters an environment where individuals focus on problem-solving rather than allocating blame. It promotes a culture of collaboration, where team members work collectively to address challenges without fear of retribution or blame.

Therefore, it's essential to cultivate a workplace atmosphere that encourages a focus on the problem at hand rather than fixating on assigning blame to individuals. A culture that prioritizes problem-solving and constructive discussions over fault-finding fosters open communication, transparency and a shared responsibility to overcome obstacles. This not only drives innovation and growth but also contributes significantly to a positive and productive work environment.

ATTITUDE AND EFFECTIVENESS

'Success or failure in business is caused more by mental attitude than by mental capacities.'

—Sir Walter Scott

Effectiveness in leadership roles is intricately linked to attitude—a factor often overlooked or undervalued. As a supervisor, manager or leader, your effectiveness is largely evaluated based on the influence your attitude exerts on the outcomes achieved. Engaging in self-reflection and posing crucial questions can shed light on how one's attitude shapes leadership.

To ascertain the impact of your attitude on your team's success, certain fundamental inquiries prove illuminating:

1. Is there factual evidence reflecting your genuine desire for the success of those under your leadership?
2. Does your behaviour demonstrate a commitment to investing ample time in planning, anticipating future needs and providing essential resources for your team?
3. Can you maintain composure during crises or emergencies, avoiding irrational reactions that might affect your team's response?
4. Do you foster an environment that encourages calculated risk-taking while refraining from penalizing bearers of unpleasant news?

5. How effectively do you handle disagreements without letting them turn into discordant interactions?
6. Do you actively avoid flaunting symbols of status or privilege that might induce fear, isolation, or suspicion among your team members?
7. Are you skilled in negotiating goals to be both challenging and achievable? Can you guide rather than command and coach instead of dictating?
8. Are you rarely caught off-guard and possess the ability to swiftly obtain necessary information? While knowing everything at all times isn't necessary, minimizing surprises and knowing where to acquire pertinent information are crucial.
9. Can you simplify complex issues and ensure your communications are easily comprehensible, minimizing instances where clarification is needed?
10. Do you encourage dissenting opinions to arrive at more comprehensive and sound decisions, acknowledging that unanimity might not always reflect a thorough examination of all aspects, akin to the practice of Alfred Sloan?

Addressing these questions and actively adjusting attitudes and behaviours based on the responses can profoundly shape your effectiveness as a leader. The willingness to introspect and adapt one's attitude fosters a conducive environment for growth, innovation and overall success within the team or organization.

Being unable to offer clear answers to these pivotal questions not only signifies a gap in self-awareness but could also suggest a lack of transparency regarding your attitudes and their impact within the organization. When key decision-makers evaluate your potential for career advancement, they rely on tangible evidence of how your attitudes shape your contributions.

Aligning your attitudes with your day-to-day actions is paramount. Your behaviour becomes a visible manifestation of your attitudes, providing a clear narrative of how you engage with tasks, colleagues and challenges. This coherence between your stated attitudes and your exhibited behaviours serves as a blueprint for others to comprehend your approach, values and commitment to the organization's goals. Therefore, ensuring that your attitudes are consistently evident in your actions becomes instrumental in building a compelling case for career advancement.

OVERCOMING YOUR OWN NEGATIVE ATTITUDES

'The greatest discovery of my generation is that a human being can alter their life by altering attitudes.'

—William James

When confronted with the realization that one's actions or attitudes contribute to an issue, it's an opportunity for growth. Here are some strategies to navigate such moments of self-realization:

1. **Reflect on Negative Attitudes:** taking a moment to scrutinize negative attitudes helps forecast their potential implications. By asking, 'Where will this lead?' individuals gain clarity about the consequences of persisting with such attitudes.
2. **Embrace Humour:** laughter serves as a powerful antidote. Its ability to alleviate stress and lighten the mood makes it an effective coping mechanism in difficult situations.
3. **Embrace Setbacks with a Positive Outlook:** acknowledging setbacks as a natural facet of life while

maintaining a positive perspective can mitigate the duration and severity of problems.

4. **Practice Self-Talk:** engaging in calming self-talk during stressful times can significantly reduce stress levels. Taking breaks, like having lunch away from work, provides valuable moments to unwind and recharge.
5. **Cultivate Positive Self-Talk:** when feeling low, encouraging oneself with positive affirmations can uplift the mood and outlook.
6. **Assess Priorities and Goals:** evaluating whether personal aspirations align with one's genuine desires or are shaped by external expectations is crucial. Authenticity in setting goals is vital for personal contentment.
7. **Simplify Matters:** simplifying complexities wherever possible streamlines decision-making and reduces unnecessary stress.
8. **Prevent Small Issues from Escalating:** nipping minor problems in the bud prevents them from snowballing into larger, more challenging issues.
9. **Strengthen Social Connections:** investing in meaningful relationships with family and friends enriches life experiences. Maintaining these bonds becomes a buffer during challenging times, requiring as much effort as dedicated to one's professional role.
10. **Collaborative Problem-Solving:** brainstorming positive solutions with others fosters a constructive approach. Considering alternative actions or words that could have yielded a more positive outcome is a valuable exercise in growth and learning.

Embarking on the journey of change and growth entails traversing a path fraught with challenges. The act of apologizing, initiating a fresh start, acknowledging one's mistakes, persistently striving and heeding advice seldom unfolds effortlessly. These endeavours demand courage, humility and resilience as they entail confronting not just one's own shortcomings but also the scepticism or disdain of others.

Navigating the terrain of avoiding errors proves daunting as some missteps seem inevitable despite our best intentions. The pursuit of sustained success presents its own set of difficulties; the allure of diversions often tests our resolve, making it arduous to remain steadfast on the path to achievement.

The arduous task of breaking free from detrimental habits, steering clear of monotonous routines, and embracing the liberating power of forgiveness requires tremendous effort. Exercising caution in our actions, taming the tempestuous nature within us and shouldering the weight of deserved blame are not endeavours for the faint-hearted.

These undertakings, while undoubtedly challenging, serve as the stepping stones to brighter tomorrows, guiding us toward a realm of personal growth, fulfilment and ultimately, a more enriched existence.

BUILD UP YOUR SELF-CONFIDENCE

'If you have a positive attitude and constantly strive to give your best effort, eventually you will overcome your immediate problems and find you are ready for greater challenges.'

— Pat Riley

Learning to believe in yourself is fundamental for fostering confidence, a trait that permeates every aspect of our lives. Your attitude, a multifaceted mirror reflecting various facets of your personality, prominently showcases your confidence.

To bolster self-assurance, addressing pivotal aspects becomes imperative. Firstly, acknowledging your limitations provides a foundation for growth. Secondly, honing the skill of decision-making contributes significantly to self-confidence. Expanding your awareness of these crucial components facilitates a robust framework for building and nurturing belief in oneself.

WHAT LIMITATIONS WILL YOU ACCEPT?

In the 1960s, Jimmy Heuga emerged as a dominant figure in the skiing world, showcasing his prowess by clinching a bronze medal in the 1964 Olympic slalom. However, at twenty-five, his disappointment was palpable when he landed an eighth-place finish in the same event in 1968. Unbeknownst to him, he was battling the onset of multiple sclerosis, a diagnosis that came as a staggering blow.

Receiving grim prognoses from several doctors who deemed his nerve damage severe enough to confine him to a wheelchair, Heuga staunchly rejected their verdict. Instead, he embarked on an unwavering journey to defy the limitations imposed by his condition. Refusing to succumb to helplessness, he adopted a rigorous routine, commuting on his bicycle, exercising and swimming daily for twenty minutes, demonstrating an unyielding spirit. Moreover, he undertook the daunting task of relearning how to ski despite the hurdles posed by his illness.

His ethos pivoted on the notion that while he could endure the confinement of a wheelchair, the idea of being idle and dependent was inconceivable. His vision centred on revitalizing his life through a robust health regimen. His straightforward philosophy resonates deeply: navigate around the disease's obstacles. He likened it to learning to swim, where initial steps involve merely getting one's feet wet, gradually wading deeper each day until confidence in swimming is gained.

This mindset not only enabled Heuga to confront and manage his illness but also galvanized him to establish the Heuga Centre. This foundation offers programs tailored from his personal experiences to assist others battling MS, serving as a beacon of hope and resilience.

Truly, his story and approach offer invaluable guidance to individuals navigating challenges, underscoring the importance of resilience, perseverance and the ability to adapt in the face of adversity.

WHAT CHOICES DO YOU MAKE?

Ann Weber, a psychologist hailing from Asheville, North Carolina, illuminates the discomfort inherent in making choices, attributing it to the weight of responsibility. She astutely points out the allure of indecision, a safe haven where blame finds no purchase. However, she emphasizes the perilous downside: a life spiralling beyond one's control.

Delving deeper into the nuances of indecision, Jane Burka, a psychologist based in Berkeley, California, delineates various personality archetypes grappling with decisiveness. The perfectionists, wary of errors, opt to evade decisions rather than risk any misstep. Non-compromisers strive for the unattainable, feeling compromised at any hint of relinquishment. Freedom lovers, faced with an array of choices, balk at commitment, perpetually seeking open-ended options. Then there are the dependents, placing greater trust in others than in their own judgment.

What strings these disparate personas together, as you might have guessed, is a common thread of lacking self-esteem, often intricately woven into their upbringing. The perfectionist might stem from a family where errors were met with harsh criticism. Dependents, too, might have been conditioned by constant admonitions about their decision-making abilities, ultimately leading to resignation.

Mike Hernacki, a writer from San Diego, echoes this sentiment, attributing his own lack of self-assurance and ensuing indecisiveness to his unforgiving upbringing. His childhood was steeped in a puritanical ethos, an environment where praise was a rarity, and any achievement fell short of absolute perfection. He reminisces about receiving stellar grades, only to be met with a dismissive, 'What's with the B?' from his father.

Hernacki reflects on a pivotal moment in his life when, despite dating the same woman for four years, he couldn't muster the courage to propose until she issued an ultimatum. His journey meandered through various career trajectories, from teaching to advertising, law and stockbroking. However, his ultimate aspiration to become a writer remained dormant for fourteen years due to a fixation on monetary gain, believing his prior professions failed to yield substantial income.

Similarly, Frank McCourt's odyssey from Ireland to the United States was fraught with adversity. Arriving penniless, unskilled, and devoid of companionship, he toiled in menial and gruelling jobs to finance his college education. Despite harbouring aspirations to write, McCourt found himself teaching English in New York City high schools. It wasn't until retirement that he found the self-assurance to pursue his writing aspirations. His debut book, *Angela's Ashes*, not only became a bestseller but also paved the way for two more critically acclaimed memoirs.

Psychologists Meryle Gillman and Diane Gage, co-authors of *The Confidence Quotient: 10 Steps to Conquer Self-Doubt*, offer counsel to the indecisive, advocating for the recognition of negative influences that have shaped their outlook. They propose a visualization exercise wherein individuals identify the doubters, like a critical parent, juxtaposed with a reinforcement figure—someone consistently supportive. This exercise aims to reframe their mental dialogue, fostering a positive alliance between doubt and encouragement. The process of making decisions becomes pivotal in this journey, showcasing that the world doesn't crumble regardless of the outcome, ultimately empowering one's sense of control.

These anecdotes collectively emphasize the profound impact of upbringing on one's confidence and decisiveness. They underscore the pivotal role played by childhood environments in shaping individuals' self-perception and approach toward decision-making, highlighting the importance of fostering an environment that nurtures self-esteem and cultivates the courage to make choices without fear of judgment or reproach.

Making strides toward becoming more decisive involves actively engaging in the process of decision-making on a daily basis. Waiting for a sense of absolute control before making choices is akin to delaying quitting smoking until the taste becomes unpleasant—an elusive scenario. Instead, initiating a series of small decisions forms the groundwork for fostering decisiveness. It's about setting a course of action and committing to it, much like saying, 'I'll take steps to quit smoking,' and then following through.

Indecisiveness often stems from apprehension about the unknown future. Yet, upon taking action, the perceived horror of these uncertainties tends to diminish. The strategy involves dissecting decisions into manageable steps. For instance, when navigating personal investments, delving into the entire stock market isn't necessary. Focus on acquiring essential knowledge about the specific investments you're interested in—a smaller, more digestible approach.

Mike Hernacki's perspective resonates profoundly here. He believes that the significance of decisions lies more in the commitment behind them than their immediate impact. Moreover, Hernacki advocates that the majority of decisions are not as pivotal as one might imagine, and very few are actually fatal. What truly matters is the dedication to making them work.

Reflecting on his own journey, Hernacki acknowledges that decision-making isn't always effortless, even now. However, having built a track record of making choices has transformed his approach. He emphasizes the transformative power of accumulating a history of decisions, which bolsters the confidence to engage actively in decision-making. This evolution signifies a shift in mindset—from hesitancy to an assertive 'getting out there and making them'

Ultimately, this approach underscores the importance of embracing a proactive stance in decision-making. It's about recognizing that the magnitude of decisions often lies in our commitment to see them through, and that taking incremental steps consistently builds the foundation for a more decisive and empowered approach to life's choices.

'Positive attitude enables us to focus not on uncontrollable events or circumstances, but on our response to them.'